Global Forum on Transparency and Exchange of Information for Tax Purposes: Korea 2020 (Second Round)

PEER REVIEW REPORT ON THE EXCHANGE OF INFORMATION ON REQUEST

This work is published under the responsibility of the Secretary-General of the OECD. The opinions expressed and arguments employed herein do not necessarily reflect the official views of OECD member countries.

This document, as well as any data and map included herein, are without prejudice to the status of or sovereignty over any territory, to the delimitation of international frontiers and boundaries and to the name of any territory, city or area.

Note by Turkey
The information in this document with reference to "Cyprus" relates to the southern part of the Island. There is no single authority representing both Turkish and Greek Cypriot people on the Island. Turkey recognises the Turkish Republic of Northern Cyprus (TRNC). Until a lasting and equitable solution is found within the context of the United Nations, Turkey shall preserve its position concerning the "Cyprus issue".

Note by all the European Union Member States of the OECD and the European Union
The Republic of Cyprus is recognised by all members of the United Nations with the exception of Turkey. The information in this document relates to the area under the effective control of the Government of the Republic of Cyprus.

Please cite this publication as:
OECD (2020), *Global Forum on Transparency and Exchange of Information for Tax Purposes: Korea 2020 (Second Round): Peer Review Report on the Exchange of Information on Request*, Global Forum on Transparency and Exchange of Information for Tax Purposes, OECD Publishing, Paris, *https://doi.org/10.1787/97daef15-en*.

ISBN 978-92-64-49315-5 (print)
ISBN 978-92-64-55375-0 (pdf)

Global Forum on Transparency and Exchange of Information for Tax Purposes
ISSN 2219-4681 (print)
ISSN 2219-469X (online)

Photo credits: OECD with cover illustration by Renaud Madignier

Corrigenda to publications may be found on line at: *www.oecd.org/about/publishing/corrigenda.htm*.
© OECD 2020

The use of this work, whether digital or print, is governed by the Terms and Conditions to be found at *http://www.oecd.org/termsandconditions*.

Table of contents

Reader's guide 5

Abbreviations and acronyms 9

Executive summary 11

Summary of determinations, ratings and recommendations 13

Overview of Korea 17
    Legal system 17
    Tax system 17
    Financial services sector 18
    Anti-money laundering framework 19
    Recent developments 20

Part A: Availability of information 21
    A.1. Legal and beneficial ownership and identity information 21
    A.2. Accounting records 50
    A.3. Banking information 56

Part B: Access to information 61
    B.1. Competent authority's ability to obtain and provide information 61
    B.2. Notification requirements, rights and safeguards 66

Part C: Exchanging information 69
    C.1. Exchange of information mechanisms 69
    C.2. Exchange of information mechanisms with all relevant partners 76
    C.3. Confidentiality 77
    C.4. Rights and safeguards of taxpayers and third parties 79
    C.5. Requesting and providing information in an effective manner 80

Annex 1: List of in-text recommendations................................ 89
Annex 2: List of Korea's EOI mechanisms 91
Annex 3: Methodology for the review 97
Annex 4: Jurisdiction's response to the review report................... 99

Reader's guide

The Global Forum on Transparency and Exchange of Information for Tax Purposes (the Global Forum) is the multilateral framework within which work in the area of tax transparency and exchange of information is carried out by over 160 jurisdictions that participate in the Global Forum on an equal footing. The Global Forum is charged with the in-depth monitoring and peer review of the implementation of the international standards of transparency and exchange of information for tax purposes (both on request and automatic).

Sources of the Exchange of Information on Request standards and Methodology for the peer reviews

The international standard of exchange of information on request (EOIR) is primarily reflected in the 2002 OECD Model Agreement on Exchange of Information on Tax Matters and its commentary, Article 26 of the OECD Model Tax Convention on Income and on Capital and its commentary and Article 26 of the United Nations Model Double Taxation Convention between Developed and Developing Countries and its commentary. The EOIR standard provides for exchange on request of information foreseeably relevant for carrying out the provisions of the applicable instrument or to the administration or enforcement of the domestic tax laws of a requesting jurisdiction. Fishing expeditions are not authorised but all foreseeably relevant information must be provided, including ownership, accounting and banking information.

All Global Forum members, as well as non-members that are relevant to the Global Forum's work, are assessed through a peer review process for their implementation of the EOIR standard as set out in the 2016 Terms of Reference (ToR), which break down the standard into 10 essential elements under three categories: (A) availability of ownership, accounting and banking information; (B) access to information by the competent authority; and (C) exchanging information.

The assessment results in recommendations for improvements where appropriate and an overall rating of the jurisdiction's compliance with the EOIR standard based on:

1. The implementation of the EOIR standard in the legal and regulatory framework, with each of the element of the standard determined to be either (i) in place, (ii) in place but certain aspects need improvement, or (iii) not in place.

2. The implementation of that framework in practice with each element being rated (i) compliant, (ii) largely compliant, (iii) partially compliant, or (iv) non-compliant.

The response of the assessed jurisdiction to the report is available in an annex. Reviewed jurisdictions are expected to address any recommendations made, and progress is monitored by the Global Forum.

A first round of reviews was conducted over 2010-16. The Global Forum started a second round of reviews in 2016 based on enhanced Terms of Reference, which notably include new principles agreed in the 2012 update to Article 26 of the OECD Model Tax Convention and its commentary, the availability of and access to beneficial ownership information, and completeness and quality of outgoing EOI requests. Clarifications were also made on a few other aspects of the pre-existing Terms of Reference (on foreign companies, record keeping periods, etc.).

Whereas the first round of reviews was generally conducted in two phases for assessing the legal and regulatory framework (Phase 1) and EOIR in practice (Phase 2), the second round of reviews combine both assessment phases into a single review. For the sake of brevity, on those topics where there has not been any material change in the assessed jurisdictions or in the requirements of the Terms of Reference since the first round, the second round review does not repeat the analysis already conducted. Instead, it summarises the conclusions and includes cross-references to the analysis in the previous report(s). Information on the Methodology used for this review is set out in Annex 3 to this report.

Consideration of the Financial Action Task Force Evaluations and Ratings

The Financial Action Task Force (FATF) evaluates jurisdictions for compliance with anti-money laundering and combating terrorist financing (AML) standards. Its reviews are based on a jurisdiction's compliance with 40 different technical recommendations and the effectiveness regarding 11 immediate outcomes, which cover a broad array of money-laundering issues.

The definition of beneficial owner included in the 2012 FATF standards has been incorporated into elements A.1, A.3 and B.1 of the 2016 ToR. The 2016 ToR also recognises that FATF materials can be relevant for carrying out EOIR assessments to the extent they deal with the definition of beneficial ownership, as the FATF definition is used in the 2016 ToR (see 2016 ToR, annex 1, part I.D). It is also noted that the purpose for which the FATF materials have been produced (combating money-laundering and terrorist financing) is different from the purpose of the EOIR standard (ensuring effective exchange of information for tax purposes), and care should be taken to ensure that assessments under the ToR do not evaluate issues that are outside the scope of the Global Forum's mandate.

While on a case-by-case basis an EOIR assessment may take into account some of the findings made by the FATF, the Global Forum recognises that the evaluations of the FATF cover issues that are not relevant for the purposes of ensuring effective exchange of information on beneficial ownership for tax purposes. In addition, EOIR assessments may find that deficiencies identified by the FATF do not have an impact on the availability of beneficial ownership information for tax purposes; for example, because mechanisms other than those that are relevant for AML purposes exist within that jurisdiction to ensure that beneficial ownership information is available for tax purposes.

These differences in the scope of reviews and in the approach used may result in differing conclusions and ratings.

More information

All reports are published once adopted by the Global Forum. For more information on the work of the Global Forum on Transparency and Exchange of Information for Tax Purposes, and for copies of the published reports, please refer to www.oecd.org/tax/transparency and http://dx.doi.org/10.1787/2219469x.

Abbreviations and acronyms

AITA	Adjustment of International Taxes Act
AML/CFT	Anti-Money Laundering/Countering the Financing of Terrorism
APG	Asia Pacific Group
AXIS system	Automatic exchange and analysis of foreign financial information system
CDD	Customer Due Diligence
DTC	Double Tax Convention
EOI	Exchange of information
EOIR	Exchange of information on request
FATF	Financial Action Task Force
FSC	Financial Services Commission
FSS	Financial Supervisory Service
Global Forum	Global Forum on Transparency and Exchange of Information for Tax Purposes
KoFIU	Korea Financial Intelligence Unit
KRW	Korean Republic won
LLC	Limited Liability company
Multilateral Convention	The Multilateral Convention on Mutual Administrative Assistance in Tax Matters, as amended
NTS	National Tax Service
TIN	Taxpayer Identification Number
VAT	Value added tax

2016 Assessment Criteria Note	Assessment Criteria Note, as approved by the Global Forum on 29-30 October 2015.
2016 Methodology	2016 Methodology for peer reviews and non-member reviews, as approved by the Global Forum on 29-30 October 2015.
2016 Terms of Reference (ToR)	Terms of Reference related to Exchange of Information on Request (EOIR), as approved by the Global Forum on 29-30 October 2015.

Executive summary

1. This report analyses the implementation of the international standard of transparency and exchange of information on request in Korea on the second round of reviews conducted by the Global Forum. It assesses both the legal and regulatory framework in force as at 28 April 2020 and the practical implementation of this framework against the 2016 Terms of Reference, including in respect of EOI requests received and sent during the review period from 1 January 2016 to 31 December 2018. This report concludes that Korea is to be rated overall **Largely Compliant** with the international standard. In 2012, the Global Forum evaluated Korea in a combined review against the 2010 Terms of Reference for both the legal implementation of the EOIR standard as well as its operation in practice (the 2012 Report). That report concluded that Korea was rated Compliant overall (refer to Annex 3).

Comparison of ratings for First Round Report and Second Round Report

Element		First Round Report (2012)	Second Round Report (2020)
A.1	Availability of ownership and identity information	LC	PC
A.2	Availability of accounting information	C	LC
A.3	Availability of banking information	C	LC
B.1	Access to information	C	C
B.2	Rights and Safeguards	C	C
C.1	EOIR Mechanisms	C	C
C.2	Network of EOIR Mechanisms	C	C
C.3	Confidentiality	C	C
C.4	Rights and Safeguards	C	C
C.5	Quality and timeliness of responses	C	C
	OVERALL RATING	C	LC

C = Compliant; **LC** = Largely Compliant; **PC** = Partially Compliant; **NC** = Non-Compliant

Progress made since previous review

2. The 2012 Report made three recommendations in respect of three essential elements: ensuring that information pertaining to holders of bearer shares is available (element A.1); clarifying that trustees of personal trusts must maintain underlying documentation (element A.2); and continuing to develop its EOI network with all relevant partners (element C.2). Korea has addressed each of these recommendations.

Key recommendations

3. The 2016 Terms of Reference contain additional requirements in respect of the availability of beneficial ownership information. Korea's AML/CFT and tax regime require collecting identity and beneficial ownership information for all legal entities and arrangements, but the legal framework established may not fully be in line with the standard. As such, Korea is recommended to ensure that beneficial ownership information for all relevant entities and arrangements is available (elements A.1 and A.3). There are also recommendations related to ensuring the availability of ownership and accounting information due to the large number of inactive companies registered with the Register Office (elements A.1 and A.2).

EOI practice

4. During the review period, Korea received 289 requests from 17 EOI partners and sent 309 EOI requests to 20 EOI partners. Peers were satisfied with their EOI relationship with Korea and reported a high quality of responses, although sometimes with delays. Peers were also satisfied with the quality of communication with Korea's EOI unit.

Overall rating

5. Korea has achieved a rating of Compliant for seven elements (B.1, B.2, C.1, C.2, C.3, C.4 and C.5), Largely Compliant for two elements (A.2 and A.3) and Partially Compliant for one element (A.1). Korea's overall rating is Largely Compliant based on a global consideration of Korea's compliance with the individual elements.

6. This report was approved at the Peer Review Group of the Global Forum meeting in July 2020 and was adopted by the Global Forum on 18 August 2020. A follow-up report on the steps undertaken by Korea to address the recommendations made in this report should be provided to the Peer Review Group of the Global Forum no later than 30 June 2021 and thereafter in accordance with the procedure set out under the 2016 Methodology.

Summary of determinations, ratings and recommendations

Determinations and Ratings	Factors underlying Recommendations	Recommendations
Jurisdictions should ensure that ownership and identity information including information on legal and beneficial owners, for all relevant entities and arrangements is available to their competent authorities *(ToR A.1)*		
The legal and regulatory framework is in place but needs improvement	While the vast majority of companies, partnerships and trusts would have an account with a Korean financial institution, which is required to keep beneficial ownership information, there is no obligation for companies, partnerships or trustees of personal trusts to engage a financial institution. The definition of beneficial ownership for companies applied by financial institutions is in line with the standard; however, the determination for partnerships follows the approach for companies, including taking a 25% threshold as a starting point which is not always in accordance with the form and structure of partnerships. For trusts, it is not clear whether information on "any other natural person exercising ultimate control over the trust" will be available. A considerable amount of information relevant for the identification of beneficial owners will be available with the tax administration; however, the scope of this information may not match the definition of beneficial owner under the standard.	Korea is recommended to ensure that comprehensive beneficial ownership information in line with the standard is available in respect of all relevant legal entities and arrangements.

Determinations and Ratings	Factors underlying Recommendations	Recommendations
Partially Compliant	There are a large number of inactive companies that maintain legal personality but are not being supervised by the tax administration. This raises concerns that legal and beneficial ownership information might not be available in all cases.	Korea is recommended to review its system, whereby a significant number of inactive companies remain with legal personality on the commercial register, to ensure that legal and beneficial ownership information is available.
Jurisdictions should ensure that reliable accounting records are kept for all relevant entities and arrangements *(ToR A.2)*		
The legal and regulatory framework is in place		
Largely Compliant	There is a large number of inactive companies on the commercial register that maintain legal personality and may not be complying with the obligation to maintain accounting records.	Korea is recommended to review its system, whereby a significant number of inactive companies remain with legal personality on the commercial register, to ensure that accounting records are available.
Banking information and beneficial ownership information should be available for all account-holders *(ToR A.3)*		
The legal and regulatory framework is in place but needs improvement	Financial institutions hold a significant amount of information on the beneficial owners of a partnership and a trust; however, the determination for partnerships follows the approach for companies, including taking a 25% threshold as a starting point which is not always in accordance with the form and structure of partnerships. For trusts, it is not clear whether information on "any other natural person exercising ultimate control over the trust" will be available.	Korea is recommended to ensure that beneficial ownership information in line with the standard is available in respect of partnerships and trusts.
Largely Compliant		

SUMMARY OF DETERMINATIONS, RATINGS AND RECOMMENDATIONS – 15

Determinations and Ratings	Factors underlying Recommendations	Recommendations
Competent authorities should have the power to obtain and provide information that is the subject of a request under an exchange of information arrangement from any person within their territorial jurisdiction who is in possession or control of such information (irrespective of any legal obligation on such person to maintain the secrecy of the information) *(ToR B.1)*		
The legal and regulatory framework is in place		
Compliant		
The rights and safeguards (e.g. notification, appeal rights) that apply to persons in the requested jurisdiction should be compatible with effective exchange of information *(ToR B.2)*		
The legal and regulatory framework is in place		
Compliant		
Exchange of information mechanisms should provide for effective exchange of information *(ToR C.1)*		
The legal and regulatory framework is in place		
Compliant	Korea had problems communicating with one EOI partner regarding the interpretation of the foreseeable relevance standard in 3.5% requests received during the review period.	Korea is recommended to continue clearly communicating with all of its EOI partners to ensure that its interpretation of the foreseeable relevance standard is consistent with Article 26(1) of the OECD Model Convention.
The jurisdictions' network of information exchange mechanisms should cover all relevant partners *(ToR C.2)*		
The legal and regulatory framework is in place		
Compliant		

Determinations and Ratings	Factors underlying Recommendations	Recommendations
The jurisdictions' mechanisms for exchange of information should have adequate provisions to ensure the confidentiality of information received *(ToR C.3)*		
The legal and regulatory framework is in place		
Compliant		
The exchange of information mechanisms should respect the rights and safeguards of taxpayers and third parties *(ToR C.4)*		
The legal and regulatory framework is in place		
Compliant		
The jurisdiction should request and provide information under its network of agreements in an effective manner *(ToR C.5)*		
Legal and regulatory framework	This element involves issues of practice. Accordingly, no determination on the legal and regulatory framework has been made.	
Compliant	Korea did not provide any status updates in the first year of the review period. Korea introduced updates to its computer system which increased the number of status updates being provided in the last year of the review period to 65%.	Korea is recommended to continue to ensure that it provides status updates in all cases where it takes over 90 days to provide a response.

Overview of Korea

7. This overview provides some basic information about Korea that serves as context for understanding the analysis in the main body of the report.

Legal system

8. The Korean legal system is a civil law system. The hierarchy of laws in Korea is as follows: (i) the Constitution laying down all fundamental rights and duties of Korean citizens and the organisation of the different powers; (ii) acts adopted by the National Assembly; (iii) Enforcement Decrees; and (iv) Enforcement Rules or Regulations. Pursuant to the Constitution, international treaties and national laws are placed on the same level. Where there is conflict between the two norms, the international treaty will always prevail over the national law. This principle is recognised in Korea's case law.

9. The Korean judicial system consists of three tiers: (i) the Supreme Court at the top; (ii) high (appellant) courts; and (iii) district courts. In tax matters, litigation is dealt with by the National Tax Tribunal and can be appealed to a district court.

Tax system

10. The administration of Korea's tax system is under the general jurisdiction of the Ministry of Economy and Finance. The National Tax Service (NTS) was established as an external organisation of the Ministry in 1966 and is mainly in charge of the assessment and collection of national taxes.

11. The NTS consists of 11 bureaus and 41 divisions at the headquarters level located in Sejong, 7 Regional Tax Offices and 125 District Tax Offices. Under the supervision of the NTS, a Regional Tax Office is responsible for the direct guidance and control over the activities of the District Tax Offices. It also has responsibilities for auditing large taxpayers. Local Tax Offices are the front-line organisation responsible for the assessment, collection, audit and investigation of all internal taxes. In general, a District Tax Office consists of

a Collection Support Division, a Revenue Control Division and Investigation Divisions. At the end of 2018, 20 368 officials work for the NTS.

12. At the national level, there are ten main taxes, including corporation tax, income tax, inheritance and gift tax and value added tax (VAT). There are also some local income taxes as well as local consumption taxes. These taxes are subject to specific sets of rules and are collected by separate local administrations.

13. A natural person resident in Korea is subject to income tax on a worldwide basis while a non-resident is taxable on income from Korean sources. The scale of rates ranges from 6% to 42% in a progressive manner. Non-incorporated partnerships are flow-through entities usually subject to the rules provided by the Income Tax Act, that is, their income is taxed within the hands of the partners.

14. Any company that is incorporated in Korea or has its seat of effective management in Korea, is subject to corporation tax on a worldwide basis. Foreign companies are taxed on their income from Korean source. The tax rate is 10% on the first KRW 200 million (EUR 147 085) of taxable income, 20% on taxable income over KRW 200 million up to KRW 20 billion (EUR 14 million), 22% on taxable income over KRW 20 billion up to KRW 300 billion (EUR 220 million) and 25% on taxable income over KRW 300 billion.

15. A tax identification number (TIN) is attributed to all taxpayers in Korea. All legal entities receive a TIN upon registration with the NTS. This TIN is kept indefinitely, even when characteristics of the entity are altered. Natural persons receive a resident registration number upon registration of their birth or, for foreigners, when they intend to reside in Korea for more than 90 days. This resident registration number is used as a TIN by the NTS.

Financial services sector

16. Korea has a well-developed financial sector, but is not a regional or international financial centre or a centre for company formation and registration. Korea's GDP in calendar year 2018 amounted to KRW 1 782 268 billion (EUR 1 312 billion), of which finance and insurance business accounted for 5.3%.

17. The principal supervisory authority of the Korean financial sector is the Financial Services Commission (FSC), which is responsible for drafting and amending financial laws and regulations and issuing regulatory licences to financial institutions. The FSC's functional responsibilities are shared among the Securities and Futures Commission, which supervises the financial markets and the Financial Intelligence Unit (KoFIU), which

is responsible for implementing Korea's AML/CFT regime. The KoFIU has delegated its supervisory powers to a number of agencies, including the Financial Supervisory Service (FSS). The FSS is responsible for carrying out AML/CFT supervision of financial institutions, including trust business operators, and conducting other enforcement and oversight activities as directed by the FSC.

18. At the end of 2018, Korea's financial sector encompassed 57 banks, 54 insurance companies, 501 financial investment services companies, 106 credit-specialised financial companies, 79 mutual savings banks and 2 237 mutual financial co-operatives.

19. In order to engage in trust business activities in Korea, the entity must be licensed by the FSC. The Trust Act and the Financial Investment Services and Capital Markets Act apply to trust business operators. As of 31 December 2019, there were 56 trust business operators (19 banks, 20 financial investment services companies, 6 insurance companies and 11 real estate trust operators).

Anti-money laundering framework

20. In Korea, only financial institutions are subject to comprehensive AML/CFT measures. Other professions, such as lawyers and accountants, are not subject to the AML/CFT framework.

21. Korea's AML/CFT legal framework comprises of a number of different laws, including the Act on Real Name Financial Transactions and Confidentiality and its Enforcement Decree (which prohibits financial transactions under false names and number accounts) and the Act on Reporting and Using Specified Financial Transaction Information and its Enforcement Decree and regulations (which set out the AML/CFT preventive measures including customer due diligence (CDD) obligations).

22. The Financial Action Task Force (FATF) and the Asia Pacific Group (APG) conducted a joint evaluation of Korea's compliance with the AML/CFT standards in 2019. In this report, Korea received a largely compliant rating on FATF Recommendation 10 for CDD of financial institutions, a compliant rating for Recommendation 11 for record keeping and a compliant rating for Recommendation 17 for reliance on third parties. Recommendation 22 was rated partially compliant as lawyers, notaries, scriveners and accountants are not subject to CDD obligations. Recommendations 24 and 25 were rated partially and largely compliant, respectively, due to beneficial ownership information not always being updated (in particular for legal entities). Korea was rated as having a moderate level of effectiveness for Immediate Outcome 5. This report was published on 16 April 2020 and is available at www.fatf-gafi.org/countries/#Korea.

Recent developments

23.   Korea committed to implement the Common Reporting Standards (CRS) for the sharing of financial account information with other CRS participating jurisdictions. Korea began exchanges under the CRS in September 2017. The 2017 Adjustment of International Taxes Act (AITA) requires businesses to submit their Country-by-Country Report (CbCR) on their business year, beginning from January 2016, to the NTS. These CbCRs have been exchanged with the tax authorities in the country of a subsidiary since 2018.

Part A: Availability of information

24. Sections A.1, A.2 and A.3 evaluate the availability of ownership and identity information for relevant entities and arrangements, the availability of accounting information and the availability of banking information.

A.1. Legal and beneficial ownership and identity information

> Jurisdictions should ensure that legal and beneficial ownership and identity information for all relevant entities and arrangements is available to their competent authorities.

25. The 2012 Report concluded that legal ownership information in respect of relevant legal entities and arrangements was in place. Korea was recommended to ensure that ownership information pertaining to bearer shares be available in all circumstances. As explained below, this issue has been resolved.

26. The 2012 Report did not raise any issues related to the practical implementation of the ownership requirements. The practical availability of ownership information continues to be supervised by the National Tax Service (NTS) and the Financial Supervisory Service (FSS). This continues to be sufficient to ensure the availability of ownership information.

27. This review covers the availability of legal and beneficial ownership information. Two recommendations are made in this respect: (i) ensure that beneficial ownership information for all relevant legal entities and arrangements is available; and (ii) ensure that legal and beneficial ownership information for inactive companies is available.

28. During the review period, Korea received 21 requests for legal and beneficial ownership and identity information and was able to respond to all of the requests that it found valid.

29. The table of recommendations, determination and rating is as follows:

Legal and Regulatory Framework			
	Underlying Factor		Recommendations
Deficiencies identified	While the vast majority of companies, partnerships and trusts would have an account with a Korean financial institution, which is required to keep beneficial ownership information, there is no obligation for companies, partnerships or trustees of personal trusts to engage a financial institution. The definition of beneficial ownership for companies applied by financial institutions is in line with the standard; however, the determination for partnerships follows the approach for companies, including taking a 25% threshold as a starting point, which is not always in accordance with the form and structure of partnerships. For trusts, it is not clear whether information on "any other natural person exercising ultimate control over the trust" will be available. A considerable amount of information relevant for the identification of beneficial owners will be available with the tax administration; however, the scope of this information may not match the definition of beneficial owner under the standard.		Korea is recommended to ensure that comprehensive beneficial ownership information in line with the standard is available in respect of all relevant legal entities and arrangements.
Determination: The element is in place, but certain aspects of the legal implementation of the element need improvement			
Practical Implementation of the standard			
	Underlying Factor		Recommendations
Deficiencies identified	There are a large number of inactive companies that maintain legal personality but are not being supervised by the tax administration. This raises concerns that legal and beneficial ownership information might not be available in all cases.		Korea is recommended to review its system, whereby a significant number of inactive companies remain with legal personality on the commercial register, to ensure that legal and beneficial ownership information is available.
Rating: Partially Compliant			

A.1.1. Availability of legal and beneficial ownership information for companies

30. The Commercial Act allows for five types of companies having legal personality to be incorporated in Korea:

- *Jusik Hoesa* (joint stock company) can be a public or private company with an unlimited number of shareholders whose liability is limited to the amount of their contributions. Shares are freely transferable.
- *Yuhan Hoesa* (limited company) is a closely held company with less than 50 members and whose shares cannot be freely transferred.
- *Hapmyong Hoesa* (general partnership company) has two of more general partners with unlimited liability.
- *Hapja Hoesa* (limited partnership company) has at least one partner with unlimited liability and at least one partner with limited liability.
- *Yuhan Chaekim Hoesa* (type of LLC) that may be established in Korea since 2012, where members' liabilities remain limited to the capital each member contributed, while their management and representation rights are equal for every member. These LLCs are subject to similar requirements as other types of companies.

31. A foreign company with a branch in Korea or a foreign company incorporated abroad but having sufficient nexus with Korea, by reason of having its place of effective management in Korea, is subject to the same commercial and tax requirements as those applicable to a similar Korean company, or if no similar form of Korean company exists, that with the closest features.

32. The 2012 Report concluded that legal ownership information in respect of companies was required to be available in line with the standard and that these rules were properly implemented to ensure availability of ownership information in practice. This continues to be the case, except in the case of inactive companies, as was also confirmed in EOI practice.

33. The main source of beneficial ownership information on companies are financial institutions as they are required to identify the beneficial owners of companies in line with the standard as part of their CDD obligations. The NTS also has a significant amount of information relevant for the identification of beneficial owners of a company.

34. The following table[1] shows a summary of the legal requirements to maintain ownership information in respect of companies:

Type	Company law	Tax law	AML/CFT law
Joint stock companies	Legal – all Beneficial – none	Legal – all Beneficial – some	Legal – all Beneficial – some
Limited companies	Legal – all Beneficial – none	Legal – all Beneficial – some	Legal – all Beneficial – some
General partnership companies	Legal – all Beneficial – none	Legal – all Beneficial – some	Legal – all Beneficial – some
Limited partnership companies	Legal – all Beneficial – none	Legal – all Beneficial – some	Legal – all Beneficial – some
LLCs	Legal – all Beneficial – none	Legal – all Beneficial – some	Legal – all Beneficial – some

Legal ownership and identity information

(a) Commercial law

35. Domestic and foreign[2] companies are required to maintain ownership information. There have been no changes to these legal obligations since the 2012 Report (see paragraphs 64-66).

36. Joint stock companies, limited companies and LLCs must maintain a share/member register at their principal office which must be in Korea. The register must be updated but Korean laws do not set out a specific time-frame; however, obligations under the commercial and tax laws ensure that the register is kept up-to-date and all information filed with the NTS is kept indefinitely. Shareholders bear responsibility to ask companies to update entries in the share registers. There is no specific penalty for shareholders not asking the company to update the entry; however, the transfer of shares is not definitive unless the transfer has been entered in the register. Upon request by the shareholder concerned, the sanction is applied by companies' supervisory authorities and can be up to KRW 5 million (EUR 3 680) and can be repeated

---

1. The table shows each type of company and whether the various rules applicable require availability of information for "all" such entities, "some" or "none". "All" in this context means that every company of this type is required to maintain ownership information in line with the standard and that there are sanctions and appropriate retention periods. "Some" in this context means that a company will be required to maintain a portion of this information under applicable law.
2. Foreign companies include branches of foreign companies and foreign companies with their seat situated abroad and their place of effective management in Korea.

multiple times until the entry is finally updated. Shareholders and creditors may inspect the register at any time during business hours.

37. Managers and directors of general and limited partnership companies are also required to keep a member register at their principal office. Further, any transfers of interest must be registered in the articles of incorporation.

38. There are no explicit provisions in the Commercial Act regarding the retention period for the articles of incorporation and the shareholder register maintained by a company, nevertheless, the Act does provide that a company's books and records, including all important documents relating to its business and liquidation, must be kept for ten years after the registration of the liquidation with the Register Office (Art. 266, Commercial Act). According to Korean officials, this implies that ownership information must be retained as long as the company exists. Further, ownership information is filed with the NTS (refer to Tax laws below) and retained indefinitely. The legal personality of a company ceases to exist, in principle, through the dissolution procedure. Dissolution of a company includes voluntary dissolution, a merger with another Korean or foreign entity, bankruptcy, and an order or judgment by the Register Office of the District Court. During this procedure, the books and records (including the share/member register) of a company must be maintained by the liquidator. Directors of the company become the liquidators, unless the articles of incorporation provide otherwise or other persons have been appointed at a meeting of shareholders, or a court has appointed a liquidator. Dissolution can take between one and five years to complete. Once the liquidation has been registered with the Register Office as completed, the company is removed from the register and the liquidator or a custodian, appointed by the court, must retain all historical books and records of the company for ten years at a location determined by the court (Art. 541, Commercial Act).

(b) Commercial registration

39. Some legal ownership information will also be available with the Register Office. There have been no changes to these legal obligations since the 2012 Report (see paragraphs 56-63). Under the Commercial Registration Act, companies, either domestic or foreign[3] companies, are required to register with the Register Office of the District Court having jurisdiction over the seat (or registered office) of the company. When registering, general and limited partnership companies provide their articles of incorporation to the Register Office, which contains identity information on the company's members. Joint-stock companies, limited companies and LLCs are not covered by this obligation; however, they are required to keep share/member registers

---

3. Foreign companies include branches of foreign companies and foreign companies with their seat situated abroad and their place of effective management in Korea.

(refer to paragraph 36). Companies are also required to provide a capital injection statement issued by a Korean financial institution. Any changes to the information filed with the Register Office must be updated within two weeks of the change. Fines up to KRW 5 million (EUR 3 680) may be imposed for a failure to comply with any of these obligations.

40. According to Article 520-2 of the Commercial Act, the Register Office must publish a public notice in the Official Gazette requiring a dormant company (i.e. one that has not communicated with the Register Office for five years) to report to the Register Office, within two months of the publication, that it has not closed its business. A company that fails to report to the Register Office within that time is deemed dissolved and three years later, unless the company applies to be reinstated with the Register Office, is deemed liquidated. In order to be reinstated, the company must refile its application and comply with any outstanding obligations. At the time of the deemed dissolution, the directors of the company become the liquidators, unless a liquidator is appointed in a shareholder meeting or a person is appointed by the court.

41. The Register Office must keep its registers and any entries in these registers permanently. Any documents pertaining to entries in these registries and submitted by the companies themselves are kept for ten years from the date of registration of the completion of liquidation.

(c) Tax laws

42. A company's legal personality only comes into effect once registered with the Register Office. Also, without being registered for commercial purposes, companies cannot apply for a business licence and register for tax purposes. Running a business requires a tax identification number (TIN) in order to be able to issue proper invoices.

43. When registering with the NTS, companies (including any foreign company having a place of effective management or a branch in Korea) must provide an incorporation report setting out ownership information, and accompanied with the articles of incorporation, a list of shareholders or members and a capital injection statement issued by a Korean financial institution. The NTS must be informed of any changes to the information set out in the incorporation report within 15 days of such change (Art. 109(3), Corporate Tax Act). General and limited partnership companies can opt for the Special Taxation for Partnership Firms which requires the identity of the company's members be provided to the NTS upon registration and updated on an annual basis.[4] Any information provided to the NTS for registration must be kept as

---

4. This regime and its implications are further described in section A.1.3 Partner information requirements.

long as it is necessary for tax purposes and at least for five years considering the statute of limitation (Art. 85-3, Framework Act on National Taxes). A penalty tax of 0.5% of the value in relation to shares may be imposed for failing to submit the list of shareholders or members when filing the incorporation report or for providing incomplete or incorrect information (Art. 75-2 Corporate Tax Act).

44. Under the Corporate Tax Act, companies must keep a share/member register. Any change in the ownership of shares that occurred during a business year must be reported by joint stock companies, limited companies and LLCs to the NTS as an enclosure to the annual tax return. In the case of listed companies, companies must report the majority shareholders (those who own at least 1% of the shares issued by the company and is the largest shareholder thereof (including shares held by his associated persons)). In the case of non-listed companies, shareholders who own more than 1% or KRW 5 million (EUR 3 680) of the shares issued by the company are to be reported. Also, under the Framework Act of National Taxes, any information reported to the NTS, including information in relation to shareholders, must be information on the persons (legal or natural) who are actually receiving the income or profit. This reporting is a snapshot in time and reflects the situation at the end of the business year. A penalty tax of 1% of the value in relation to shares may be imposed for failing to submit the list of shareholders or members or for providing incomplete or incorrect information (Art. 75-2 Corporate Tax Act). When a taxpayer does not submit information or is suspected to have made false representation, the NTS may order the taxpayer to submit the information or conduct a tax investigation. A penalty of up to KRW 20 million (EU 14 727) may be imposed on a taxpayer who fails to comply or makes a false statement in response to a NTS inquiry (Art. 88, Framework Act on National Taxes). As indicated above, information relevant for tax purposes must be kept for at least five years considering the statute of limitation, and this also applies in the case of a liquidated company.

45. Pursuant to Article 160-5 of the Income Tax Act, a person required to adopt double-entry bookkeeping must have a business account with a Korean financial institution. This account must be used for the settlement of a payment made through a financial institution in relation to the purchase and supply of goods and services, or the receipt or payment of salaries and rental fees. The NTS must be informed of this account as well as any changes to this account or the opening of a new business account. Article 131-2 of the Enforcement Decree of the Income Tax Act lists those persons subject to double-entry bookkeeping, including business owners whose annual income reaches a certain amount depending on the industry (i.e. KRW 600 million (EUR 448 375) for retail or wholesale business, KRW 300 million (EUR 224 187) for manufacturing, restaurant, lodging, financial or insurance business, and KRW 150 million (EUR 112 093) for real estate leasing

business or other personal service business) and business operators eligible for tax credits, tax reductions or income deductions under the Restriction of Special Taxation Act. Korean officials advise that most companies retain local accounts in order to comply with the tax law, but statistics are not publicly available.

46. To conclude, the obligation to maintain legal ownership information for domestic and foreign companies under the commercial and tax law continues to be in line with the standard.

Beneficial ownership information

47. The standard was strengthened in 2016 and beneficial ownership information on companies should be available.

AML/CFT laws

48. Korean financial institutions are generally the main source of beneficial ownership information. Although companies may engage lawyers, notaries, scriveners or accountants, these persons are not subject to the AML/CFT laws.

49. The Act on Real Name Financial Transactions and Confidentiality requires that financial institutions perform financial transactions (including account opening) with customers under their real name. The Act on Reporting and Using Specified Financial Transaction Information, its Enforcement Decree and AML/CFT Regulations set out the AML/CFT preventative measures, including CDD obligations, record keeping requirements and sanctions.

50. Article 5-2 of the Act on Reporting and Using Specified Financial Transaction Information require financial institutions to undertake CDD measures of a customer and the actual owner when: establishing a business relationship; conducting an occasional transaction or through several related transactions; there is a suspicion of money laundering or the financing of terrorism; or there are doubts about the veracity or adequacy of the CDD documentation. The actual owner means the natural person who ultimately owns or controls, directly or indirectly, the customer or the person on whose behalf a transaction is being conducted. This concept of beneficial ownership came into effect on 1 January 2016.

51. Article 10-5 of the Enforcement Decree to the Act on Reporting and Using Specified Financial Transaction Information sets out how actual owner(s) are to be identified. First, it reinforces the concept that the actual owner is the natural person who ultimately owns or controls the customer or who promises or agrees to conduct a financial transaction (including account opening) under his/her real name. A financial institution is required to

identify and verify the identity of the actual owner. If the customer is a legal person or arrangement, then the actual owner(s) is:

   a. the person who owns at least 25% of the issued and outstanding voting shares or other equity interest in the legal person or arrangement
   b. if the institution cannot verify the identity of a person in a), then the person who meets any of the following:
      i. holds the largest portion of shares or other equity interest in the legal person or arrangement;
      ii. has appointed the majority of representatives, managing partners, executives, etc. solely or by agreement, contract, etc. with the other shareholders, partners, etc.; or
      iii. ultimately controls the legal person or arrangement if he/she is clearly different shareholders, partners, etc. under (i) or (ii);
   c. if no such person in a) or b) exists or can be identified, then the natural person who holds the position of senior managing official.

52. Korean government officials and representatives of financial institution met during the on-site visit interpret "if the institution cannot verify the identity of a person in a)" to mean that if there are doubts as to whether the person identified in step a) is the beneficial owner or where no person is identified under step a), then the institution must move to step b). Korea should clarify the terms "if the institution cannot verify the identity of a person" to ensure that financial institutions apply the procedures for identifying and verifying the actual owner(s) of a company in line with the standard (refer to Annex 1).

53. Article 10-5 also clarifies that where a legal person or arrangement is identified at step a) or b) of the identification procedure, the financial institution must look through the legal person or arrangement to identify the natural person(s) ultimately exercising ownership or control. The Article further clarifies that it may be possible for more than one natural person to be identified as an actual owner.

54. A financial institution must verify the customer and actual owner's identity using reliable, independent source documents, data or information, etc. (Art. 10-4, Enforcement Decree and Art. 37, AML/CFT Regulations). Identity information includes name, date of birth, gender, identification number, country of citizenship and address. Financial institutions will generally verify information using the national registration system[5] or the national registries of legal persons (maintained by the Register Office).

---

5. All residents in Korea receive a resident registration number which is issued by the government at birth. Foreign nationals residing in Korea for over 30 days

55. A financial institution must also understand and obtain information on the purpose and intended nature of the business relationship, as well as the nature of the customer's business and its ownership and control structure (Art. 37, AML/CFT Regulations). Further, the institution must verify the identity and authority of any person acting on behalf of the customer (Art. 38, AML/CFT Regulations). Article 38 of the AML/CFT Regulations set out the type of information that is to be collected in order to conduct CDD.

56. Financial institutions are required to conduct ongoing CDD throughout the course of the business relationship with the customer by examining all aspects of the customer's transactions to determine whether the transactions are consistent with the institution's knowledge of the customer, the customer's business, risk profile and source of funds. Institutions are also required to review existing CDD documentation to ensure that the information is up to date and adequate (Art. 34, AML/CFT Regulations). There is no specific minimum timeframe set out in the AML/CFT laws for the update, rather financial institutions are to undertake updates within an "appropriate time" according to the level of risk associated with the customer. An "appropriate time" refers to: (i) when a transaction raises concerns regarding ML/FT; (ii) the CDD legal requirements change; (iii) there is a material change in the way an account is operated; or (iv) there are doubts about the accuracy of the customer's CDD information (Art. 25, AML/CFT Regulations). According to the FSS and representatives from Korean financial institutions, in practice, financial institutions review their high-risk customers annually and non-high-risk customers are reviewed every three years.

57. As financial institutions conduct ongoing CDD following a risk-based approach, the beneficial ownership information may not be up to date at all times. The reliance on CDD alone may not be sufficient to meet the standard that requires the information to be adequate, accurate and up to date; this concern may be partly addressed by requirements under the tax law (see below), nevertheless, Korea should take measures to ensure that available beneficial ownership information is kept up to date at all times (refer to Annex 1).

58. All records obtained through CDD measures, account files and business correspondence and the results of any analysis undertaken must be kept for at least five years after the termination of the business relationship (Art. 84, AML/CFT Regulations).

59. Financial institutions verify the identity of customers and beneficial owners according to risk-based procedures. Financial institutions may apply simplified CDD measures by not verifying the identity of the actual owner(s)

---

are required to register with the relevant district office within 14 days after the determination of their domicile.

of the state or a local government; an exhaustive list of public organisations; other financial companies (excluding casino operators and persons identified as high risk by the KoFIU); or a listed company (Art. 10-5(5), Enforcement Decree). Article 30 of the AML/CFT Regulations provides that enhanced CDD must be conducted if the customer is high-risk. This Article sets out a list of what is to be considered as high-risk, including a customer that is a trust or other similar vehicle; a non-resident customer from a country that has insufficient AML/CFT systems or measures in place, or the institution considers that the level of risk involved is such that enhanced CDD should apply; the customer is a company with nominee shareholders or shares in bearer form; the FATF makes an official request to the FIU; non face-to-face customers; or other circumstances determined by the Commissioner of KoFIU. Enhanced CDD requires enhanced scrutiny of a customer's identity, the source of funds and transaction monitoring (Art. 42, AML/CFT Regulations).

60. If a financial institution is not satisfied with the identification information received from a customer or is unable to obtain the information, the institution must not open an account, commence the business relationship, or perform the transaction, and must send a report to the FIU (Art. 5-2, Act on Reporting and Using Specified Financial Transaction Information). A financial institution may delay completion of the customer verification if the delay is essential to maintaining the normal course of business, where the risks of money laundering or terrorist financing are effectively managed and verification occurs as soon as practicable afterwards (Art. 10-6, Enforcement Decree and Art. 33, AML/CFT Regulations).

61. Financial institutions may rely upon third parties to perform CDD measures on their behalf, if certain conditions are met but the ultimate responsibility for the CDD measures are with the relying institution (Art. 53 and 54, AML/CFT Regulations). The conditions for third party reliance are that: (i) the relying institution must be satisfied that the third party is regulated, supervised and has measures in place to comply with the CDD requirements; (ii) the relying institution must immediately obtain from the third party the CDD information required by the AML/CFT laws; and (iii) the relying institution must take adequate steps to satisfy itself that copies of the identification data and other relevant information relating to the CDD requirements will be made available without delay. According to Korea Federation of Banks representatives, banks in Korea do not rely on third parties to perform CDD, rather the banks will carry out CDD measures for non-bank financial institutions.

62. An administrative fine of up to KRW 100 million (EUR 73 635) may be imposed on a financial institution officer who fails to comply with the CDD requirements (Art. 17, Act on Reporting and Using Specified Financial Transaction Information).

Tax laws

63. As explained in paragraph 44, when filing annual returns, companies are obligated to provide information on their majority shareholders (for listed companies) or those owning more than 1% or KRW 5 million (EUR 3 680) of the shares (for non-listed company). If shareholders can transfer economic benefits derived from dividends on a contractual basis, companies are required to pay dividends subject to taxation to the person that actually receives the benefit (Art. 14, Framework Act on National Taxes). As such, companies must report information on persons (legal or natural) who actually receive the income, profit, property, etc. and not "nominal owners" if there are some. Further, under the Inheritance and Gift Tax Act, a gift tax is imposed when property (for instance, shares) for which title has been registered under the name of a person other than the actual owner. This information along with other information contained in the tax database, such as information obtained through the observance of tax filing obligations, during tax audits or from government and third party's sources, provides the NTS with a considerable amount of information which may go beyond identifying the legal owners of a company; however, beneficial ownership information as defined under the standard will not be fully available.

64. Article 31 of the Adjustment of International Tax Act (AITA) allows the NTS to obtain any information from any person for domestic tax and EOI purposes. According to NTS officials, this included obtaining beneficial ownership information. In order to make this Article clear, and ensure consistency with the international standard, it was amended, effective 1 January 2020, to provide that "any information" includes beneficial ownership information. Article 31-4 was also amended to impose an administrative fine not exceeding KRW 30 million (EUR 22 090) on any person that fails to comply with a request for information from the NTS. NTS officials interpret Article 31 as indirectly requiring companies to maintain beneficial ownership information (refer to discussion below).

65. The Enforcement Decree of the AITA was also amended, effective 11 February 2020, to set out the definition of beneficial owner. According to Article 47(11) of the Decree, for purposes of a company, the beneficial owner has the same meaning as actual owner set out in Article 10-5 of the Enforcement Decree to the Act on Reporting and Using Specified Financial Transaction Information (refer to paragraph 51). This definition is in line with the standard.

Discussion and conclusion

66. The AML/CFT requirements described above ensure the identification of beneficial owners of companies in line with the standard. A specific obligation for beneficial ownership information to be available in line with the standard covers only those companies that engage a financial institution.

As provided in paragraphs 39 and 43, in order to incorporate and apply for a business licence, a company must provide the NTS with a capital injection statement issued by a Korean financial institution. This guarantees that, at least at the time of incorporation, beneficial ownership information will be available through the CDD obligations of the financial institution. Additionally, certain companies must maintain a business account with a Korean financial institution in order to comply with obligations under the tax laws (refer to paragraph 45). There is, however, no legal obligation on all companies to engage a financial institution throughout the lifetime of the company. Consequently, if a company (not required to maintain a business account) closes its account in Korea and opens an account in a foreign country during its lifetime, up-to-date beneficial ownership information on that company may no longer be available in Korea. Korean officials advise that most companies retain local accounts in order to comply with the tax law, but statistics are not publicly available.

67. The recent enactments to the AITA bring the definition of beneficial owner into the tax law. Although Article 31 of the AITA provides access power to the NTS to obtain beneficial ownership information, it does not impose an explicit obligation on companies to maintain such information. Further, there is no clear obligation in the tax law providing for the systemic and comprehensive collection and maintenance of up-to-date beneficial ownership information in line with the standard. NTS officials maintain that existing obligations (i.e. to file a list of any changes in share ownership during the year and to report those persons that actually received income, profit, etc. (refer to paragraph 44)) ensure that up-to-date information on a company's beneficial owners is available. While these obligations ensure that a company has up-to-date information on its owners, which may go beyond its legal owners, it is not clear that these obligations ensure that a company keeps information on its beneficial owners in line with the standard.

68. In conclusion, it is noted that the scope of AML/CFT coverage of companies is arguably significant as most of them would be expected, for both practical business reasons and to comply with the tax law, to maintain a bank account in Korea. Nonetheless, it is recommended that Korea take measures to ensure that identification of beneficial owners of companies is available in Korea as required under the standard.

Supervision of obligations to maintain legal and beneficial ownership information

69. The 2012 Report concluded that legal requirements on the availability of legal ownership of companies were properly implemented in practice. There have not been any significant changes made to the supervisory and enforcement practice.

70. The Register Office, the NTS and the FSS carry out supervisory and enforcement measures. The FSS supervises financial institutions to ensure compliance with the AML/CFT laws. The FSS carries out very robust supervisory activities which ensures the availability of legal and beneficial ownership information. Refer to element A.3 below for more information.

Register Office

71. When a new registration application is received either electronically or in hard-copy, a Register Office staff will check that relevant documents have been submitted and verify the identity of any persons mentioned as shareholder or member in the company's articles of incorporation or application form. Verification of identity is done using the resident registration number (refer to paragraph 15) and other public sources of information. When an application is approved, the applicant is given the registration documents that must be submitted to the NTS (refer to paragraph 75). It generally takes the Register Office 1.5 to 2 days to register a company.

72. Register Office officials advise that the level of compliance with registration requirements is high considering the necessity to be registered in order to obtain legal personality and apply for a business licence with the NTS.

73. The Register Office does not carry out on-site visits to ensure compliance; however, it will conduct an investigation into a company if it receives a request for an investigation or receives information regarding potential non-compliance from interested parties. As mentioned in paragraph 36, a shareholder bears responsibility to ask a company to update the register and the transfer of shares is not definitive unless the transfer has been entered in the register. As such, a shareholder may notify the Register Office if a company fails to update its register and sanctions may be imposed on the company. During the review period, the Register Office carried out 56 inspections and imposed 28 penalties.[6] This would include a shareholder claiming that a company's share register is not up to date.

74. Further, the Register Office requires any company from which it has not received any information over the last five years (i.e. a dormant company) to contact the Register Office. This is to verify whether the company is still conducting business. If no response is received, the company is deemed dissolved and, after three years, unless the company applies to be reinstated, is deemed liquidated. In order to be reinstated, the company must refile its application with the Register Office and comply with any outstanding

---

6. Note that it is not possible to specify the type of Commercial Code violations for which these penalties were imposed.

obligations (refer to paragraph 40). In practice, Korean officials advise that approximately 35 000 companies are deemed dissolved each year. Although these companies may not have contacted the Register Office over the last five years, any information filed with the Register Office and the NTS is kept indefinitely. Further, these companies have an obligation to maintain the books and records during the period of dormancy and deemed dissolution, as well as for ten years after the date of liquidation.

National Tax Service

75. When registering, the NTS will verify the information provided by the applicant. Identity is verified using the resident registration number (refer to paragraph 15), the Register Office's register, or other databases maintained by government authorities. The NTS also has a broad database which facilitates verification that suspicious activities are not being conducted (for instance name borrowing[7]).

76. Once the application meets the criteria, the licence is issued immediately. However, if this is not the case, then a NTS officer will go through the submitted information with the applicant. If any suspicious activities (i.e. name borrowing) are detected, the NTS officer may decide that additional verification is required, in which case the officer may request additional documentation or conduct an on-site inspection. During an on-site inspection, the NTS officer will visit the applicant's place of business and take measures to identify the legal and beneficial owners of the company. Depending on the circumstances, the issuance of a licence can be delayed from three to eight days. Licences may also be refused for a number of reasons, such as additional verification documentation not being provided. The refusal of a business licence has no impact on a company's registration with the Register Office. During the review period, the NTS refused to issue licences in very few cases and there were a small number of cases where applicants withdrew their licence applications.

77. According to NTS officials, the level of compliance with the licensing and registration requirements is very high because companies require a TIN in order to conduct business (i.e. issuing invoices). The NTS also carries out on-site visits to ensure that companies running a business are licensed. During the review period, the NTS found 144 businesses operating without a valid licence. The NTS registered and assessed taxes on the unreported income for these businesses, in addition to imposing a penalty tax.

---

7. Name borrowing is when an individual opens an account in his/her own name and subsequently allows a third party to use the account.

78. The NTS also verifies that licensed companies are conducting business by visiting a company's place of business and interviewing the company's representatives. When a company is clearly no longer conducting business, the NTS will deregister the company by cancelling the company's TIN so that it may no longer legally conduct business in Korea. That company will still appear in the NTS' database as a company no longer carrying on business and all relevant information remains available in the database. The NTS does not share this information with the Register Office which raises concerns regarding the availability of ownership information for inactive companies (refer to paragraph 83). During the review period, more than 200 000 companies were deregistered.

79. All domestic companies and foreign companies with taxable income in Korea must annually file corporate tax returns. The NTS tax database tracks the filing of returns on a real time basis and all returns are automatically examined as part of the official tax assessment. NTS officials advise that the tax filing compliance rate for companies in 2018 was 96%. In cases where returns are not filed by the due date, either a reminder or, depending on the taxpayer's past filing compliance record, a fine warning is sent. If returns are still not filed despite the reminders/warnings, the NTS takes strong deterrent actions. Enforcement actions such as estimating taxpayer's income to issue an estimated tax bill and imposing fines for non-filing are taken to ensure the filing of the outstanding return. Non-filing of a return may also trigger an on-site visit to the company's place of business to ensure that the company is still conducting business.

80. The NTS carries out an extensive audit programme. Each Division within the NTS (Corporate Tax, Income Tax, VAT and Property Tax) conducts its own audits to verify compliance with the various tax laws. Audits include on-site and off-site inspections. There are two types of audits: random audits (i.e. taxpayers are randomly selected to be audited) and targeted audits (i.e. a taxpayer has failed to comply with the law or has acted suspiciously resulting in an audit being launched). Each Division has identified areas or taxpayers that are high-risk or require additional monitoring. All audits include verifying that ownership records are kept. As the supervisory activities are conducted by Regional and District Tax Offices, it is not possible to provide statistics regarding the number of on-site visits or audits conducted.

81. NTS officials advise that in 2018, approximately 0.6% of companies were audited by the Investigation Division, while in 2017 and 2016, 0.7% and 0.8% of companies were audited by this Division. Also, during the review period, penalties were imposed against non-compliant taxpayers, including penalties under the Corporate Tax Act for the non-filing of a tax return (approximately KRW 101 558 million (EUR 74 783 066)), the under-reporting

of income (approximately KRW 576 444 million (EUR 424 469 266)), and the failure to make entries in books.[8]

82. In addition to the supervisory activities described above, the NTS carries out numerous preventative programmes, public relations programmes and educational seminars. For instance, the NTS keeps the public updated on filing tax returns and payment deadlines, all NTS-provided services, amendments to the tax laws, as well as the tax latest news through a variety of media (including newspapers, television, radio, internet and mobile applications). The NTS and its regional and district offices also hold seminars for taxpayers in various formats and the National Tax Officials Training Institute holds tax law classes for taxpayers.

Inactive companies

83. The table below sets out the number of companies registered with the Register Office (as of 31 May 2019), the NTS (as of 31 December 2018) and the difference in the number of companies registered with these authorities:

	Joint stock companies	Limited companies and LLCs	General partnership companies	Limited partnership companies	Foreign companies
Register Office	1 056 084	82 869	2 486	15 389	5 533
NTS[a]	731 140	36 615	946	3 835	1 930
Difference	324 944	46 254	1 540	11 554	3 603

Note: a. Source: 2019 National Tax Statistics.

84. There is a large discrepancy between the number of companies registered with the Register Office and those registered with the NTS. According to Korean officials, there are a few reasons to explain this discrepancy. First, the statistics provided by the Register Office are from the end of May 2019 whereas the statistics provided by the NTS are from the end of December 2018. Second, some companies registered with the Register Office have not yet applied for a business licence because they are not yet ready to commence business. Third, the NTS may have refused to issue a business licence to a company registered with the Register Office, or the applicant may have withdrawn its application. The NTS does not inform the Register Office if an application for a business licence has been refused or withdrawn. Finally, the Register Office's statistics include those companies that have not yet completed the dissolution process. According to Korean officials, there is little concern regarding inactive companies because these companies are effectively prevented from conducting

---

8. Note that the numbers are consolidated.

business in Korea. It is possible, through the NTS website, to determine whether a company, registered for tax purposes, is carrying on business in Korea (refer to paragraph 78). Note that the information on the website is currently only available in Korean.

85. Conversely, because inactive companies retain legal personality (by virtue of remaining on the Register Office's registry), there is concern that they may conduct business (including ownership changes) outside the view of the Korean authorities. For instance, there may be cases in which an entity continues to hold assets or conduct transactions entirely abroad without the need to engage with the Korean financial system, other Korean entities, or with Korean authorities and does not maintain or file updated ownership information subject to supervision. Although inactive companies are not per se inconsistent with the standard, they should be expected to keep registers up-to-date. It is acknowledged that changes to legal ownership only take effect once a transfer of shares has been entered in the register; however, as described in paragraphs 39 and 73, only some legal ownership information, not including shareholder information, is provided to the Register Office and the Register Office carries out limited supervisory measures. Therefore, if an inactive company is no longer in communication with the Register Office, the availability of adequate, accurate and up-to-date legal ownership information may not be assured. Further, as these companies are not carrying on business in Korea or engaged a Korean financial institution, the availability of adequate, accurate and up-to-date beneficial ownership information may also not be assured. This concern is mitigated because any dormant company (i.e. one that has not communicated with the Register Office for five years) is deemed dissolved and, after three years, is deemed liquidated (i.e. removed from the register), thereby removing this company's legal personality (refer to paragraph 40). Nevertheless, Korea is recommended to review its system whereby a significant number of inactive companies remain with legal personality on the Register Office's register to ensure the availability of legal and beneficial ownership information.

86. During the review period, Korea received 19 requests related to inactive companies and was able to provide information that was available within the NTS database and information obtained from financial institutions; however, there is no certainty regarding the accuracy of the information exchanged.

Conclusion and availability of ownership information in practice

87. The availability of legal ownership information in Korea is primarily ensured by the requirement to keep an up-to-date shareholder register and obligations under the tax laws. The supervisory and enforcement mechanisms carried out by the NTS generally ensures the availability of such information.

The limited supervision carried out by the Register Office does raise concerns, particularly with respect to inactive companies; however, its register is a complementary source of legal ownership information.

88. Financial institutions are generally the main source of beneficial ownership and supervision of financial institutions in respect of their compliance with AML/CFT obligations is robust (refer to element A.3). The NTS also maintains a significant amount of information that may be relevant for the identification of beneficial owners of companies; however, this information may not match the definition of beneficial owner as used in the ToR. The supervisory and enforcement mechanisms carried out by the NTS generally ensures the availability of such information.

89. During the review period, Korea received 21 requests for legal and beneficial ownership and identity information related to companies and was able to respond to all of the requests that it found valid. Peer input received confirms that this information was available and no issues were raised in this respect. One peer indicated that it did not receive the requested identity information (refer to section C.1. below).

Nominees in Korea

90. Korean law does not recognise the concept of nominee ownership, but this activity is not prohibited. However, shareholders must register their own names in order to exercise voting rights or to receive dividends and financial institutions may only perform financial transactions (including opening an account) with customers in their real name (refer to the 2012 Report, paragraphs 91-93). Additionally, under the Act on Reporting and Using Specified Financial Transaction Information, financial institutions, as part of the CDD measures, must take measures to determine if a customer is acting on behalf of any other persons, in which case any person acting as a nominee would be identified. These provisions adequately ensure the availability of accurate ownership information.

91. During the review period, Korea did not receive any requests with respect to nominees. No peers raised any concerns.

A.1.2. Bearer shares

92. The 2012 Report (paragraphs 97-103) concluded that although the Commercial Act allowed non-listed joint stock companies to issue bearer shares, there were multiple mechanisms ensuring that ownership information of such shares was kept by the company itself and available to the NTS. The report did find, however, that there was no mechanism ensuring that this information would be available in all circumstances (e.g. on an ongoing basis or when the holder of bearer shares would not be interested in claiming a

dividend or participating in the management of the company), as such, Korea was recommended to address this issue.

93. Effective 20 May 2014, the Commercial Act was amended to abolish bearer shares. There were no transitional measures or timing of registration of such shares included in the amendments. Therefore, all shares must be registered and recorded in the company's share register in order for shareholders to exercise any rights. According to Korean officials, this amendment had very little impact on joint stock companies because bearer shares had rarely, if ever, been issued in the past. According to several studies,[9] Korean companies did not issue bearer shares because managers and directors would not want to lose control of the company's management and holders had to deposit their share instruments with the company in order to exercise their rights in the company. The NTS and the FSS have never come across a non-listed company with bearer shares. The Register Office does not have any records of a company's articles of association providing the possibility of issuing that bearer shares. This legislative amendment addresses the recommendation.

94. In practice, Korea has never received a request for information regarding companies with bearer shares.

A.1.3. Partnerships

95. Jurisdictions should ensure that information is available to their competent authorities that identifies the partners in, and the beneficial owners of, any partnership that (i) has income, deductions or credits for tax purposes in the jurisdiction, (ii) carries on business in the jurisdiction or (iii) is a limited partnership formed under the laws of that jurisdiction.

96. The 2012 Report (paragraphs 104-118) concluded that partner information on partnerships was in line with the standard. There have been no relevant changes to this legal framework since that Report. However, since 2012 a new form of limited partnership (*Hapja Johap*) may be established in Korea. The partner information requirements for this partnership are the same as those applicable to partnerships reviewed in the 2012 Report.

97. Korean law provides for three types of partnerships: (i) *Johap* where each partner has unlimited liability; (ii) *Ikmyong Johap* where parties agree that one of them will make a contribution towards the business and the partners will divide any accruing profits between themselves (note that the *Ikmyong Johap* itself cannot carry on business); and (iii) *Hapja Johap* which

---

9. See "Introduction to the Commercial Act" (Choi Ki-Wan, Professor at Seoul National University); "Lecture on the Commercial Act" (Lee Cheol-Song, Professor at Hanyang University) (unofficial translation of titles and authors' names.

consists of general and limited partners. Partnerships in Korea do not have any legal personality. Foreign partnerships are subject to the same requirements as domestic partnerships. At the end of 2018, there were approximately 300 000 partnerships registered with the NTS.

98. The standard was strengthened in 2016 and beneficial ownership information on partnerships is required to be available. A considerable amount of information relevant for the identification of beneficial owners of a partnership will be available under the tax and AML/CFT laws.

Partner information requirements

99. A partnership is not required to register with the Register Office; however, it must apply for a business licence as a joint business from the NTS. When applying for a licence, the partnership must provide partner information to the NTS and any changes to this information must be reported on a yearly basis (Art. 100-16, Restriction of Special Taxation Act).

100. A partnership and its partners are treated as one "joint business" under Article 2-2 of the Income Tax Act (unless the partnership opts for the special regime, explained in the paragraph below). The partnership is therefore not required to file a tax return; rather each partner must file an annual tax return and the managing partner must also include information regarding the profit or loss allocation to each partner.

101. Partnerships (as well as general partnership companies and limited partnership companies) may opt for the Special Taxation for Partnership Firms pursuant to Article 100-15 of the Restriction of Special Taxation Act which allows the partnership to be treated as a flow through entity where tax is exempt at the level of the partnership, but each partner is subject to pay and file taxes on earned income from the partnership. If the partner is a non-resident, income distributed from the partnership will be subject to withholding tax in Korea. To opt for the special regime, a partnership must file an application with NTS and provide partner information. Partnerships must then annually submit a statement of profit or loss with the NTS. Each partner is also required to file its own annual tax return with the NTS.

102. Under the tax laws, each partner is required to maintain records for five years after the end of the tax period to which it relates and regardless whether the partnership ceases to exist. Further, any information filed with the NTS is kept indefinitely.

103. The availability of partner information for domestic and foreign partnerships under the tax law continues to be in line with the standard.

Beneficial ownership information

104. Although partnerships may engage lawyers, notaries, scriveners, or accountants, these persons are not subject to the AML/CFT laws. There is no requirement for all partnerships to maintain a bank account in Korea during the lifetime of the partnership. As discussed in paragraph 45, partnerships subject to double-entry bookkeeping requirements must have a business account with a Korean financial institution and keep the NTS informed of such account. According to Korean officials, most partnerships maintain a business account with a Korean financial institution in order to comply with the tax law, but statistics are not publicly available. Where a partnership has engaged a financial institution, then the AML/CFT law would require the financial institution to carry out CDD procedures (refer to section A.1.1). All records obtained through CDD measures, account files and business correspondence and the results of any analysis undertaken must be kept for at least five years after the termination of the business relationship.

105. Under the AML/CFT law, a partnership is treated as a "customer organisation", and the definition of beneficial ownership in respect of companies applies to partnerships. As set out in paragraph 51, financial institutions are required to identify and verify the identity of those natural persons owning at least 25% of the equity interest in the partnership. If no such person exists, then the institution is to verify the identity of the natural person holding the largest portion of equity interest in the partnership, or if no person can be identified, then the natural person exercising control over the partnership. Finally, if no such person exists, the financial institution must identify those persons who hold the position of senior managing officials of the partnership as beneficial owners and verify their identity accordingly. With these rules, Korea has taken the approach of treating partnerships as legal persons for AML/CFT purposes, even though they do not have legal personality in Korea. Partnerships fall within the scope of legal persons under the definition of this term as contained in the Glossary of the FATF Recommendations,[10] and partnerships established under Korean law indeed seem to fall within this definition. As with all legal persons other than companies, the principle that should then be applied to partnerships is that the determination of beneficial ownership should take into account the specificities of their different forms

---

10. FATF (2012-19), *International Standards on Combating Money Laundering and the Financing of Terrorism & Proliferation*, FATF, Paris, France. The definition of the term legal persons is as follows: "*Legal persons* refers to any entities other than natural persons that can establish a permanent customer relationship with a financial institution or otherwise own property. This can include companies, bodies corporate, foundations, anstalt, partnerships, or associations and other relevantly similar entities.".

and structures.[11] By taking the approach to apply the same rules to partnerships as to companies, the difference in organisational structure between these two entities is not sufficiently taken into account.

106. In respect of *Johap*, all partners are jointly and severally liable for the debts of the partnership. The management of the partnership affairs is decided by a majority of the partners (Art. 706, Civil Act). The level of a partner's control does not appear to depend on their contribution to the partnership. This is a fundamental difference with companies, where the shareholders by default have voting rights at the shareholders' meetings based on their respective percentage of the capital contributions. It is for this reason that applying the same approach for a company to a *Johap* does not sufficiently take into account the form and structure of the partnership. Instead, it would be more appropriate to, for example, always consider all partners as beneficial owners when they are natural persons, and the beneficial owners behind the corporate partners should also be identified. Depending on the circumstances of each particular case, there could also be other persons exercising ultimate effective control over the *Johap* who should be considered beneficial owners

107. A *Hapja Johap* is similar to a limited partnership where the general partners control the day-to-day operations of the partnership, while the limited partners are largely passive investors with a right to review the management of the partnership and its financial matters. As is the case for *Johap*, the concept of control through ownership is not present in the legal framework for *Hapja Johap*, since it does not link control to the capital contributions made by the partners. Applying the same approach for companies to *Hapja Johap* does therefore also not sufficiently take into account the form and structure of this type of partnership.

108. Under the tax law, each partner of a partnership must file a tax return. When the partner is a corporate partner, it must file a corporate tax return and provide information on, in the case of listed companies, shareholders who own at least 1% of shares issued by the company, or, in the case of non-listed companies, any shareholder holding more than 1% or KRW 5 million (EUR 3 680) of shares issued by the company. Further, under the Framework Act of National Taxes, any information reported to the NTS must be information on the persons (legal or natural) who are actually receiving income, profit, etc. from the partnership. This information may be relevant for the identification of beneficial owners of a partnership.

109. Recently enacted provisions to the AITA clarify that the NTS may obtain beneficial ownership information from any person for domestic tax and EOI purposes, and introduce a definition of beneficial owner (refer to paragraphs 64-65). According to the definition, a beneficial owner of a partnership

---

11. See paragraphs 16 and 17 of the Interpretive Note to FATF Recommendation 24.

is the same as an actual owner set out in Article 10-5 of the Enforcement Decree to the Act on Reporting and Using Specified Financial Transaction Information (refer to paragraph 105). As explained, in paragraphs 105 to 107, by taking the approach to apply the same rules to partnerships as to companies, the difference in organisational structure between these two entities is not sufficiently taken into account.

110. Also, while these recent enactments bring the definition of beneficial owner into the tax law, as described in paragraph 65, there is no explicit obligation in the tax law providing for the systemic and comprehensive collection and maintenance of up-to-date beneficial ownership information. According to NTS officials, the annual tax filing obligations on partners ensures that up-to-date information on a partnership's beneficial owners is available. While these obligations ensure a significant amount of ownership information is available, it is unclear that beneficial ownership information, as required under the standard, will be maintained, in particular regarding partners that are legal entities or arrangements.

111. This gap, however, appears to be relatively small. First, according to NTS officials, very few registered partnerships have a corporate partner and almost all of those corporate partners are themselves registered with the NTS.[12] This means that the information collected by the NTS will typically include identification of individuals behind the corporate partners. Second, according to the Korean authorities, most partnerships only carry on domestic business. For instance, approximately 70% of partnerships registered with the NTS are engaged in real estate lease or development, and by law these partnerships may only conduct business within Korea. Finally, according to Korean officials, most partnerships do maintain a business account with a Korean financial institution in order to comply with tax law obligations, but statistics are not publicly available.

112. Although a considerable amount of information relevant for the identification of beneficial owners of a partnership will be available with the NTS and financial institutions, it is recommended that Korea ensure that comprehensive beneficial ownership information in line with the standard is available in respect of partnerships.

Supervision of obligations to maintain partner and beneficial ownership information

113. The 2012 Report did not identify any issues with respect to the supervisory measures undertaken to ensure the availability of relevant information. There have been no changes in Korea's practice in this respect.

---

12. Statistics are not publicly available.

114. All tax returns are reviewed by the NTS and additional documentation may be requested, if needed. During the review period, fines were applied on taxpayers that failed to file a return or failed to report income. It is not possible for the NTS to calculate the tax compliance rate of individuals; however, NTS officials advise that the rate is high. More information regarding the NTS' supervisory measures are described in section A.1.1 above.

115. The FSS monitors financial institutions to ensure compliance with the AML/CFT laws (refer to section A.3 below).

Availability of information in practice

116. During the review period, Korea did not receive any EOI requests related to a partnership. No peers raised any concerns.

A.1.4. Trusts

117. Two types of trusts may exist in Korea: personal trusts and business trusts. A personal trust is a legal relationship where a settlor transfers a specified property to a trustee who accepts the trust to manage such property in the interest of a beneficiary. There is nothing preventing foreign personal trusts from operating in Korea, being managed in Korea or having beneficiaries resident in Korea. The purpose of a business trust, according to the Financial Investment Services and Capital Markets Act, is to manage the assets of investors. A business trust must be managed by a licensed trust business operator, which must be a financial institution licensed by the FSC.

118. The 2012 Report determined that the information on the settlor, trustee(s) and all beneficiaries of personal trusts and business trusts would be available.

119. The standard was strengthened in 2016 and beneficial ownership information on trusts is required to be available. Information on most beneficial owners of a trust will be available if a financial institution is engaged.

120. As of December 2018, there were 56 licensed trust business operators in Korea managing more than 8 million business trusts. There is no trust register in Korea, therefore it is not possible to know the number of personal trusts (domestic and foreign); however, Korean authorities estimate that there are few, if any, personal trusts in Korea.[13]

---

13. This estimate is based on the opinion of Korean trust experts

Identification of settlor, trustee and beneficiaries

121. The Trust Act applies to personal trusts (domestic and foreign) and business trusts. Business trusts activities are also regulated under the Financial Investment Services and Capital Markets Act.

122. There is no registration requirement for personal trusts in Korea; however, when Korean law provides for the registration of certain assets and such assets are transferred to a trust, the trust deed must be filed with the appropriate government authority. As such, trust deeds pertaining to real estate, securities, or bonds must be registered. When registering, an applicant must provide information regarding the settlor, trustee and beneficiaries, and any change to this information must be immediately updated in the register.

123. The trustee of a personal trust must know the identity of any settlor and beneficiary in order for the trustee to fulfil his/her duty under the law. There have been no changes to this legal framework since the 2012 Report (paragraphs 132-133).

124. Pursuant to the AML/CFT law, financial institutions are required to know the identity of the settlor, trustee(s) and beneficiaries (paragraphs 134-135 and 142-145 of the Report). There have been no changes to this legal framework since that report. All records obtained through CDD measures, account files and business correspondence and the results of any analysis undertaken must be kept for at least five years after the termination of the business relationship.

125. There is no obligation for a personal or business trust or a trustee to be registered for tax purposes. However, when a settlor of a personal or business trust has designated another person as a beneficiary of property placed in trust, this transfer is considered a gift and must be reported to the NTS (Art. 82, Inheritance Tax and Gift Tax Act). To ensure the correct application of tax, the person handling trust matters must submit the particulars of the trust, including identification of the settlor and beneficiaries, to the NTS. This obligation covers all personal and business trusts managed by a trustee resident in Korea, even when no beneficiaries, settlors, or assets are located in Korea, as well as trusts governed by the laws of Korea or administered in Korea. A trustee cannot enjoy any benefit from the trust and must manage the assets from the trust separately from its own assets (Art. 29, Trusts Act). Any income accruing from trust property is directly attributed to the beneficiaries and tax is withheld at the time the income is attributed to the property. When a payment is made to a beneficiary, the trustee is responsible for withholding taxes corresponding to the income paid and must file a statement of payment with the NTS detailing the names of the beneficiaries. A beneficiary receiving trust income is also required to file a return with the NTS. In addition, under the Framework Act on National Taxes, any information reported to

the NTS must include information on the persons who actually receive the income or profit from the trust. Finally, the AITA was amended the AITA clarify that the NTS may obtain ownership information from any person for domestic tax and EOI purposes (see below). A taxpayer (i.e. the trustee and beneficiary) is required to maintain records for five years after the end of the tax period to which it relates and regardless whether the trust ceases to exist. Sanctions apply in the case of non-compliance.

126. Korea's legal and regulatory framework continues to ensure that information on the settlor, trustee(s) and all beneficiaries of personal trusts and business trusts will be available.

Beneficial ownership information

127. There are no obligations under the Trust Act for the beneficial owners of a trust to be identified.

128. A financial institution that is engaged by a personal trust or acts as a business trust operator is required to carry out CDD pursuant to the AML/CFT law. Article 5-2 of the Act on Reporting and Using Specified Financial Transaction Information requires a financial institution to identify and verify the natural person(s) who ultimately own or control the customer. Article 10-5 of the Enforcement Decree on the Act on Reporting and Using Specified Financial Transaction Information specifies how to identify the actual owner(s) of a legal arrangement (refer to paragraph 51) which is consistent with the definition of beneficial owner under the standard. This Article also clarifies that a financial institution must look through the legal person or arrangement to identify the natural person(s) ultimately exercising ownership or control (refer to paragraph 52).

129. Article 38(2) of the AML/CFT Regulations came into effect on 1 July 2019 to provide that the identity of the settlors, trustees, protector and beneficiaries of a trust must be verified. The Regulations are silent with respect to identifying "any other natural person exercising ultimate control over the trust". Korean authorities advise that those who exercise ultimate control over the trust are the settlors or beneficiaries of a trust and where the settlor and/or beneficiary is a legal person, the financial institution must identify the beneficial owner (natural person) of the said legal person. According to the Korean authorities, this should catch most of the situations of "any other natural person exercising ultimate control over the trust". While this may be the case for business trusts, Korea should ensure that all beneficial owners of all trusts are identified in line with the standard.

130. Recent amendments to the AITA clarify that the NTS may obtain beneficial ownership information from any person for domestic tax and EOI purposes (refer to paragraph 64). The Enforcement Decree of the AITA was

also amended, effective 11 February 2020, to clarify that the beneficial owner of a trust includes: settlors, trustees, protector, beneficiaries, and any other natural person exercising ultimate control over the trust. This definition is consistent with the standard.

131. As explained in sections A.1.1 and A.1.3, although these enactments bring the definition of beneficial owner into the tax law, there is no explicit obligation in the tax law providing for the systemic and comprehensive collection and maintenance of up-to-date beneficial ownership information in line with the standard. It is noted that currently it may be very rare for a personal trust to operate in Korea (though there have been a few cases where a foreign trust has been used for tax crimes), nevertheless, Korea is recommended to ensure that all beneficial owners of trusts are identified in line with the standard.

Supervision of obligations to maintain identity and beneficial ownership information

132. The 2012 Report did not identify any issues with respect to the supervisory measures undertaken to ensure the availability of relevant information. There have been no changes in Korea's practice in this respect.

133. Trusts with obligations under the tax laws are supervised by the NTS in the same manner as described in section A.1.1 above.

134. Business trust operators are supervised by the FSS. Within the FSS there is a business trust supervisory team, which works with the other FSS's supervisory teams in carrying out off-site and on-site inspections. For off-site inspections, FSS examiners analyse the financial and operational reporting documents submitted by business trust operators. On-site inspections are carried out on a risk-based assessment. High-risk business trust operators are inspected annually, whereas, others are inspected every three to five years.[14] An on-site inspection is carried out by five to seven examiners and takes ten business days. The examiners randomly select an operator's client files to review to ensure that CDD documentation is being maintained. In 2016, the FSS conducted 23 on-site inspections focused on AML/CFT compliance, 27 inspections in 2017 and 20 in 2018.[15] According to FSS officials,

---

14. The KoFIU and FSS carry out a comprehensive assessment of the status of implementation of an AML/CFT programme by financial institutions annually. Financial institutions must submit the results of their client assessments to the KoFIU and FSS. This information and an evaluation of the risk of an institution's clients determines whether an institution is inspected annually or not.
15. The number of inspections include those carried out on financial institutions (note that in 2018, 11 out of the 20 inspections were carried out on trust operators).

compliance with CDD obligations is very high. In cases of non-compliance, there are a range of sanctions that the FSS may impose. For further explanation of the FSS's supervisory activities and licensing of trust business operators refer to element A.3 below.

Availability of ownership information in practice

135. Korea received one request for beneficial ownership information regarding a trust during the reviewed period and was able to fully respond. No peers raised any concerns.

A.1.5. Foundations

136. Foundations can only be set up either for charitable purposes or for public benefit purposes and are, consequently, carefully monitored and scrutinised by Korean authorities. Identity of founders and donors as well as information on directors is available to government authorities, District Courts and the NTS. A foundation is typically a non-profit organisation, but it can carry on limited business activity for achievement of its purpose; however, benefits flowing from this secondary activity can only be used for non-profit purposes and cannot be distributed as such to private persons. There have been no changes to the legal framework since the 2012 Report (paragraphs 149-163).

137. Foundations do not constitute relevant entities for the standard if they meet the following criteria, which are met in the case of Korean foundations:

- object of the foundation: the foundation must have a non-profit activity/be in the public interest/have no commercial purpose
- beneficiaries: the foundation has no identifiable beneficiaries
- distribution: the foundation does no distribution to its members/founders. All of its assets and liabilities are transferred to a public body or the State upon dissolution
- irreversibility: the transfer of assets is irreversible
- tax exemption: the foundation may be exempt from tax if certain conditions are met
- government oversight: the foundation's constitution is subject to government approval.

138. At the end of 2018, there were approximately 7 000 foundations registered with the NTS. Korea did not received any EOI requests related to a foundation during the review period and no peers raised any concerns.

A.2. Accounting records

> Jurisdictions should ensure that reliable accounting records are kept for all relevant entities and arrangements.

139. The 2012 Report concluded that the legal and regulatory framework and its implementation in practice generally ensure the availability of accounting information in line with the standard; however, Korea was recommended to ensure that the legal framework clearly provided that trustees of personal trusts be required to maintain underlying documentation. Korea has addressed this recommendation.

140. The 2012 Report did not raise any issues related to the practical implementation of accounting requirements. The practical availability of accounting information continues to be supervised mainly by the National Tax Service (NTS) and is sufficient to ensure the availability of accounting information for companies and partnerships. A new recommendation, however, is made on the relatively large number of inactive companies which may not comply with the obligation to maintain up-to-date accounting information.

141. The Ministry of Finance and the Financial Supervisory Service (FSS) also carry out supervisory activities to ensure that trustees of personal trusts and business trust operators are complying with their obligations. The FSS's activities are sufficient to ensure the availability of accounting information for business trust operators.

142. During the review period, Korea received 126 requests for accounting information and was able to respond to all of the requests that it found valid.

143. The table of recommendations, determination and rating is as follows:

Legal and Regulatory Framework	
Determination: The element is in place	
Practical Implementation of the standard	
Underlying Factor	**Recommendations**
Deficiencies identified There is a large number of inactive companies on the commercial register that maintain legal personality and may not be complying with the obligation to maintain accounting records.	Korea is recommended to review its system, whereby a significant number of inactive companies remain with legal personality on the commercial register, to ensure that accounting records are available.
Rating: Largely Compliant	

A.2.1. General requirements and A.2.2. Underlying documentation

Companies

144. Under the Commercial Act and tax laws, a company and the directors of joint stock and limited liability companies are required to maintain accurate and reliable accounting records (including underlying documentation) that correctly explain all transactions, enable the financial position of the company to be determined with reasonable accuracy at any time and allow financial statements to be prepared. Further, Article 33 of the Commercial Act requires accounting records to be kept for ten years from the date of the closing of the books and five years for underlying documentation. Companies are also required to maintain accounting records for five years after the tax-filing due date for the tax year concerned under the tax laws. In addition, all companies filing an annual tax return must join to its report a balance sheet and a profit-and-loss account. This obligation applies whether the company has profits, losses, or no income. No changes to the legal framework have been made since the 2012 Report (paragraphs 182-187, 202 and 208).

145. A company that ceases to exist must maintain its accounting records for five years after the tax-filing due date for the tax year concerned. Also, all documents filed with the NTS are kept indefinitely. Additionally, under the Commercial Act, a liquidator or a court appointed custodian must keep all historical books and records, including liquidation documents, of a liquidated company for ten years after the registration of the completion of liquidation at a location determined by the court.

146. The accounting record keeping obligations of a *Yuhan Chaekim Hoesa* (a LLC) are the same as those set out in the paragraphs above.

147. When a foreign company has its place of effective management in Korea, the company is regarded as a domestic company and subject to the same accounting record keeping obligations under the tax laws applicable to a domestic company.

148. Failure to comply with these obligations is subject to a range of penalties under the Framework Act on National Tax, the Income Tax Act, the Corporate Tax Act and the Punishment of Tax Evaders Act.

Partnerships

149. The 2012 Report (paragraph 189) concluded that neither the Civil Act nor the Commercial Code contained record keeping obligations for partnerships. There were, however, obligations under the tax laws.

150. Effective 1 September 2012, Article 85-3 of the Framework Act on National Tax requires all partners to keep the books and records related to

all transactions as prescribed by each tax-related Act for five years after the tax-filing due date regardless whether the partnership ceases to exist. Article 160 of the Income Tax Act was amended in 2013 and requires any resident who has business income or any non-resident who has a domestic place of business in Korea to keep accounting records and underlying documents for five years after the tax-filing due date. In addition, the statement of financial position, a profit-and-loss statement, an account statement and other relevant documents must be submitted with the annual tax return (Art. 70, Income Tax Act). Further, any information filed with the NTS is kept indefinitely. Sanctions may be applied in the case of non-compliance.

151. Under the Restriction of Special Taxation Act, a joint business recognised as a partnership is deemed to be a single domestic corporation and provisions of the Corporate Tax Act will apply, including the obligation to maintain accounting records and file an income statement with the NTS (refer to paragraphs 144-145). Sanctions may be applied in the case of non-compliance.

152. When a foreign partnership has its head or main office in Korea and conducts business in Korea, the partnership is regarded as a domestic partnership and subject to the same accounting record keeping obligations under the tax laws applicable to a domestic partnership.

Trusts

153. In the case of a trust managed by a business trust operator, under the Financial Investment Service and Capital Market Act, operators must maintain the trust's accounting records and underlying documentation, including a list of the trust property, financial statements and accompanying statements and a full statement of management of the trust property, for ten years from the termination of the trust. In addition, an auditor must audit all trust business entities accounts within two months of the end of the fiscal year and the audit report is made available to beneficiaries and supervisory authorities. Business trust operators themselves must also keep reliable accounting records in accordance with the Commercial Act and the Corporation Tax Act. Taxpayers are required to maintain records for five years after the end of the tax period to which it relates and regardless whether the trust ceases to exist. No change to this legal framework has been made since the 2012 Report (paragraphs 191-193, 204 and 209).

154. The 2012 Report concluded that a trustee of a personal trust was required to keep accurate and reliable accounting records in line with the standard; however, it recommended that Korea clarify the law to ensure that underlying documentation in relation to personal trusts was maintained. Amendments to the Trust Act were enacted in 2014 to address this recommendation.

155. Article 39 of the Trust Act provides that the trustee of a personal trust must keep books and other documents relating to the trust affairs and ensure the clear accounting of the affairs pertaining to the trust. Pursuant to Article 3 of the Enforcement Decree of the Trust Act, the books and other documents (which include "the property lists and the specifications annexed thereto, financial statements and the specifications annexed thereto and detailed statement of the management of the trust property") must be kept for ten years from the termination of the trust. This Article does not expressly mention underlying documentation, but according to Korean officials, "other documents" is interpreted to mean that all documents relevant to a trust must be maintained, including underlying documents, such as contracts, invoices, etc. Korean officials also explain that as there are different types of trust, the listing of specific documents in the law might result in some documents being excluded from being subject to retention requirements. A trustee who is negligent in performing his/her duties of preparing, preserving and keeping books and records may be subject to an administrative fine not exceeding KRW 5 million (EUR 3 680) (Art. 146, Trust Act).

156. As the Trust Act and the Enforcement Decree are not explicitly clear regarding the obligation to maintain underlying documentation, Korea should ensure that underlying documentation, as required under the standard, is being maintained (refer to Annex 1).

Supervision of obligations to maintain accounting information

157. The 2012 Report did not raise any issues related to the practical implementation of accounting requirements.

158. The implementation of accounting requirements is ensured mainly through supervisory activities carried out by the NTS. As discussed above, the NTS tax database tracks the filing of returns on a real time basis and the tax filing compliance rate for companies in 2018 was 96%. In cases where returns are not filed by the due date, either a reminder or, depending on the taxpayer's past filing compliance record, a fine warning is sent. If returns are still not filed despite the reminders/warnings, the NTS takes strong deterrent actions. Non-filing of a return may also trigger an on-site visit or the launch of an audit. Companies (including business trust operators) and partnerships are required to annually file accounting information (i.e. balance sheet and profit-and-loss statement, etc.) with the NTS. All tax returns, including accounting records, are automatically examined as part of the official tax assessment and any taxpayer who is suspected of omitting information will be asked to provide an explanation. Also, if deemed necessary, a tax investigator may visit a taxpayer's place of business or a tax audit may be launched.

159. In addition, the NTS carries out an extensive audit programme, as described in paragraph 80. Each division within the NTS (Corporate Tax, Income Tax, VAT and Property Tax) conducts audits to verify compliance with the various tax laws. Each division has identified issues or taxpayers that are high-risk or require additional monitoring. All audits include verifying that accounting records are kept and accurate. Supervisory activities are conducted by Regional and District Tax Offices, therefore it is difficult to provide statistics on the number of on-site visits and audits conducted each year. When a division has conducted an on-site visit or an audit, and tax evasion or another significant matter is identified, the case is transferred to the Investigation Division. NTS officials advise that in 2018, approximately 0.6% of companies and 0.07% of individuals were audited by the Investigation Division; in 2017, 0.7% and 0.08% of companies and individuals were audited by this Division; and in 2016, 0.8% and 0.09% of companies and individuals were audited by this Division.[16] Further, during the review period, penalties and additional taxes were imposed under the Corporate Tax Act for the non-filing of a tax return (approximately KRW 101 558 million (EUR 74 783 066)), the failure to provide verifying documents, the failure to submit receipts (approximately KRW 134 800 million (EUR 98 809 578)) and the under-reporting of income (approximately KRW 576 444 million (EUR 424 469 266)).[17] Penalties and additional taxes were also imposed under the Income Tax Act and VAT Act on those taxpayers that failed to file a return, file verifying documents or maintain records.

160. The high filing rate, the obligation to annually file accounting information, the audit programme and the enforcement measures undertaken by the NTS are sufficient to ensure the availability of accounting information for companies and partnerships registered with the NTS.

161. The Ministry of Justice is responsible for enforcing of Trust Act for personal trusts, while the FSS supervises trust business operators. The Ministry of Justice does not carry out on-site visits but will carry out investigations when it receives referrals or complaints from interested parties. According to Ministry officials, when a referral or complaint is received, the Ministry will assess whether there is any potential non-compliance with respect to accounting records. During the review period, the Ministry did not receive any referrals or complaints relating to trustees and no administrative penalties were imposed on trustees for failing to maintain accounting records. One possible explanation is that, as noted in section A.1.4, it is very rare for a personal trust to operate in Korea (although there have been a few cases where a foreign trust has been used for tax crimes). The requirement for

---

16. Supervisory activities are conducted by Regional and District Tax Offices; accordingly the statistics from each office have been consolidated.
17. Note that the numbers are consolidated.

trustees to maintain accounting records for personal trusts is a relatively new requirement and although there may be very few personal trusts (domestic and foreign) currently being managed in Korea, this number may increase in the future. Korea should therefore monitor the compliance of trustees to maintain accounting records and underlying documentation (refer to Annex 1).

162. Business trust operators must have all of their trust accounts audited. Further, as described in paragraph 134, operators are subject to off-site and on-site inspections by the FSS. As part of the off-site inspection, the FSS will examine the operator's financial statements and the audit performed while it inspects the auditor's report. During an on-site, examiners will review the operator's client files to ensure that the accounting records are being maintained. FSS officials advise that compliance is found to be very high. For further information relating to the FSS's supervisory activities refer to element A.3 below.

Inactive companies

163. As explained in paragraphs 83 and 85, there is a substantial number of inactive companies (i.e. those registered with the Register Office but not registered with the NTS) which maintain their legal personality (approximately 64%). As explained in section A.1.1, the Register Office conducts limited supervisory measures; however, according to Korean officials, there is little concern because the large majority of these companies are in fact completely inactive and there are no transactions to be recorded in the accounting records. Further, the NTS carries out on-site visits to ensure that a company running a business is licensed, and where it is found not to be licensed, the NTS registers the company and assesses taxes on the unreported income, in addition to imposing a penalty tax. Nevertheless, up-to-date accounting information for inactive companies may not be available. There is concern that these companies may conduct business outside the view of the Korean authorities, for instance by continuing to hold assets or conducting transactions entirely abroad without the need to engage with the Korean financial system or, other Korean entities. As inactive companies do not carry out business in Korea, they would not trigger any tax liabilities and therefore may fall outside the supervisory scope of the NTS. The amount of inactive companies gives rise to concerns about the availability of accounting information. This concern is reduced because, as discussed in paragraph 40, any dormant company (i.e. one that has not communicated with the Register Office for five years) is deemed dissolved and after three years, unless the company applies to be reinstated, is deemed liquidated. In order to be reinstated, the company must refile its application with the Register Office and comply with any outstanding obligations. In practice, approximately

35 000 companies are deemed dissolved each year. Nevertheless, Korea is recommended to review its system whereby a significant number of inactive companies remain with legal personality on the commercial register to ensure the availability of accounting information.

Availability of accounting information in practice

164. During the review period, Korea received 126 requests related to accounting information and underlying documentation (including requests for financial statements, customer ledgers, account books including expenses for specific purposes and documentary evidence) for companies. Korea was able to respond to all of the requests that it found valid. Peer input received confirms that accounting information was available, although one peer indicated that it did not receive the requested accounting information (refer to discussion in section C.1.1 below).

A.3. Banking information

> Banking information and beneficial ownership information should be available for all account-holders.

165. The 2012 Report concluded that banks' record-keeping requirements and their implementation in practice were in line with the standard. Korea's AML/CFT laws continue to include comprehensive obligations on banks to verify the identity of their clients and maintain accurate records of their transactions.

166. The standard was strengthened in 2016 requiring the availability of beneficial ownership information of account-holders to also be assessed. Beneficial ownership information on companies will be available with banks. In the case of partnerships and trusts, banks will identify most beneficial owners; however, not all beneficial owners will be identified as required under the standard.

167. In Korea, banks and trust business operators are licensed by the Financial Services Commission (FSC) and supervised by the Financial Supervisory Service (FSS). The supervisory measures undertaken by the FSS adequately ensure the availability of banking information in Korea.

168. During the review period, Korea received 77 requests for banking information and was able to respond to all of the requests that it found valid.

169. The table of recommendations, determination and rating is as follows:

Legal and Regulatory Framework		
	Underlying Factor	**Recommendations**
Deficiencies identified	Financial institutions hold a significant amount of information on the beneficial owners of a partnership and a trust; however, the determination for partnerships follows the approach for companies, including taking a 25% threshold as a starting point which is not always in accordance with the form and structure of partnerships. For trusts, it is not clear whether information on "any other natural person exercising ultimate control over the trust" will be available.	Korea is recommended to ensure that beneficial ownership information in line with the standard is available in respect of partnerships and trusts.
Determination: The element is in place, but certain aspects of the legal implementation of the element need improvement		
Practical Implementation of the standard		
Rating: Largely Compliant		

A.3.1. Record-keeping requirements

170. The 2012 Report concluded that banks' record keeping obligations and their implementation in practice are in line with the standard. There has been no change to the relevant provisions or practice since that report.

171. Under the AML/CFT laws, banks are required to carry out CDD measures on their customers and maintain all identification and verification records, as well as financial transaction records for at least five years after the termination of the business relationship. An administrative fine of up to KRW 100 million (EUR 73 635) may be imposed on a person who fails to comply with these requirements (Art. 17, Act on Reporting and Using Specified Financial Transaction Information).

172. Article 5-2 of the Act on Reporting and Using Specified Financial Transaction Information requires a bank to identify and verify the natural person(s) who ultimately own or control the customer (refer to section A.1.1 above). Article 10-5 of the Enforcement Decree on the Act on Reporting and

Using Specified Financial Transaction Information sets out how beneficial owner(s) are to be identified (refer to paragraph 51).

173. Using Article 10-5, banks will identify the beneficial owners of companies in line with the standard, although, as noted in paragraph 52, Korea should clarify the terms "if the institution cannot verify the identity of a person" to ensure that banks apply the procedures for identifying and verifying the actual owner(s) of a company in line with the standard (refer to Annex 1).

174. As described in paragraph 105, banks are required to identify and verify the identity of those natural persons owning at least 25% of the equity interest in the partnership. If no such person exists, then the institution is to verify the identity of the natural person holding the largest portion of equity interest in the partnership, or if no person can be identified, then the natural person exercising control over the partnership. Finally, if no such person exists, the financial institution must identify those persons who hold the position of senior managing officials of the partnership as beneficial owners and verify their identity accordingly. By taking the approach to apply the same rules to partnerships as to companies, the difference in organisational structure between these two entities is not sufficiently taken into account. It is recommended that Korea ensure that all beneficial owners of partnerships are identified in line with the standard.

175. For trusts, Article 38(2) of the AML/CFT Regulations, which came into effect on 1 July 2019, clarifies that the identity of the settlors, trustees, protector and beneficiaries must be verified. The Regulations are silent with respect to identifying "any other natural person exercising ultimate control over the trust", as required under the standard. Korean authorities advise that those who exercise ultimate control over the trust are the settlors or beneficiaries of a trust and where the settlor and/or beneficiary is a legal person, the financial institution must identify the beneficial owner (natural person) of the said legal person. According to the Korean authorities, this should catch most of the situations of "any other natural person exercising ultimate control over the trust". Nevertheless, it is recommended that Korea ensure that all beneficial owners of trusts are identified in line with the standard.

176. Banks' CDD obligations generally ensure that most beneficial owners of legal entity and arrangement account-holders will be identified. There is a small gap identified at paragraphs 56 and 57 relating to the timing of ongoing CDD. As noted in those paragraphs, the AML/CFT laws do not set out a specific timeframe as to when CDD information is to be updated, and although Korean financial institutions conduct ongoing CDD following a risk-based approach, the beneficial ownership information may not be up to date at all times. Korea should take measures to ensure that available beneficial ownership information is kept up to date at all times (refer to Annex 1).

Supervision of obligations to maintain banking information

177. In order to carry out banking or trust business activities in Korea, an entity must be licensed by the FSC. At the end of 2018, there were 57 banks in Korea.

178. The KoFIU carries out numerous educational activities to ensure that banks, as well as the general public, are kept updated on obligations under the banking and AML/CFT laws. For instance, when the concept of beneficial ownership was introduced in 2016, the KoFIU issued numerous press releases, held monthly meetings with working-level representatives from the banking sector to educate them on the new CDD obligations and carried out promotional activity (such as public relations video clips, posters and a public contest for AML/CFT slogans) to explain to the public the importance and necessity of the AML/CFT laws. Also, 28 November has been designated as the "AML/CFT Day" in Korea to raise public awareness.

179. Banks are supervised by the FSS. The FSS' supervisory measures include off-site and on-site inspections. All banks are required to file quarterly financial and operational reports with the FSS. The FSS analyses these reports and uses this information, along with assessments provided by the KoFIU, the national risk assessment and the results of its own supervisory activities to inform its application of the risk-based assessment approach to supervision.

180. In addition to off-site inspections, FSS examiners perform full-scope and targeted on-site inspections of banks. Full-scope inspections evaluate the overall financial, management, operational and compliance performance of the bank. The selection of banks that are to undergo a full-scope inspection is made in advance during the annual examination planning held with the KoFIU. The FSS conducted 7 full-scope inspections in 2016, 15 in 2017 and 3 inspections between January and May 2018. A targeted inspection is limited in scope and is intended to address a narrow range of supervision matters, such as AML/CFT compliance and concerns, such as incidents of irregularity and unsound business activity. There is a team within the FSS that focuses only on AML/CFT compliance. This AML/CFT team conducted 23 targeted inspections in 2016, 27 in 2017 and 20 in 2018.[18]

181. A bank will be notified ten days in advance of an on-site inspection, although inspections may take place without prior notice. Four FSS examiners will attend an on-site inspection, which takes approximately ten days to complete. Customer record-keeping practices are examined during the course of an on-site inspection. FSS examiners randomly select client files to review

---

18. The number of targeted inspections include those carried out on trust business operators.

in order to determine whether the bank is complying with their CDD obligations. Following the inspection, the FSS examiners meet with the bank's management and board of directors to communicate any issues identified. The FSS examiners prepare an examination report detailing the inspection findings that include corrective actions to be taken to address any deficiencies. For more serious violations, enforcement actions are recommended. The report is subject to internal review by the FSS and the FSC. Once approved, the report is delivered to the bank.

182. Banks are required to submit an action plan for addressing the deficiencies identified in the report and report on measures taken. The reporting time depends on the severity of the identified deficiencies, but may be required on a monthly basis. The FSS will arrange high-level meetings with the bank's management if the bank fails to complete the remedial actions in a timely manner.

183. According to FSS officials, deficiencies discovered during the inspections are generally remedied within a short period. The FSS can apply a range of remedial measures on banks for non-compliance, including issuing corrective orders, giving warnings or cautions, partially or fully suspending a licence, applying administrative sanctions to senior management and employees, such as recommendation of dismissal, suspension of duties, salary reduction and reprimand. Only the KoFIU has the power to impose monetary sanctions. In 2016, the FSS AML/CFT team issued 74 remedial measures; 84 measures in 2017 and 113 measures in 2018 on banks. The KoFIU also imposed monetary sanctions on four banks for not complying with CDD obligations.

184. The supervisory measures undertaken by the FSS adequately ensures the availability of banking information in Korea.

Availability of banking information in practice

185. During the review period, Korea received 77 requests for banking information (including requests for account opening applications, ownership information of account-holders and bank statements) and was able to respond to all of the requests that it found valid. Peer input received confirms that banking information was available and no issues were raised in this respect. One peer indicated that it did not receive the requested information in one instance (refer to discussion in section C.1.1 below).

Part B: Access to information

186. Sections B.1 and B.2 evaluate whether competent authorities have the power to obtain and provide information that is the subject of a request under an EOI arrangement from any person within their territorial jurisdiction who is in possession or control of such information; and whether rights and safeguards are compatible with effective EOI.

B.1. Competent authority's ability to obtain and provide information

> Competent authorities should have the power to obtain and provide information that is the subject of a request under an exchange of information arrangement from any person within their territorial jurisdiction who is in possession or control of such information (irrespective of any legal obligation on such person to maintain the secrecy of the information).

187. As concluded in the 2012 Report, the NTS has broad access powers to obtain all types of relevant information, including ownership, accounting and banking information from any person both for domestic tax purposes and in order to comply with obligations under Korea's EOI agreements. There has been no changes to the law since that report. The NTS' access powers can be used for EOI purposes, regardless of domestic tax interest and the procedure for obtaining information when the EOI request is of civil or criminal nature are the same. In the case of failure to provide the requested information, the NTS has adequate powers to compel the production of information.

188. Korean EOI officials have access to the NTS' internal database, which contains all taxpayer-related information and other government databases, including information maintained by the Register office, the real estate register and customs information.

189. The NTS' access powers are effectively used in practice and no issue arose during the period under review. Peers were satisfied by the timeliness of the provision of the requested information and the NTS has not faced any difficulties in collecting the requested information.

190. The table of recommendations, determination and rating is as follows:

Legal and Regulatory Framework
Determination: The element is in place
Practical Implementation of the standard
Rating: Compliant

B.1.1. Ownership, identity and banking information and B.1.2. Accounting records

191. The NTS has broad access powers to obtain all types of relevant information including ownership, accounting and banking information from any person, both for domestic tax purposes and in order to comply with obligations under Korea's EOI agreements. There were no changes to the legal framework discussed in the 2012 Report (paragraphs 239-246); although one clarification amendment to the tax law was implemented, effective January 2020, which provides that the NTS may obtain beneficial ownership information from any person for domestic tax and EOI purposes, and a "beneficial owner" definition was added to the law (refer to paragraphs 64-65).

192. The NTS may question persons or examine the accounts, books, or any documents held by a taxpayer or any person who possesses or controls the information related to the concerned taxpayer (Art. 122, Corporate Tax Act; Art. 170, Income Tax Act; Art. 84 Inheritance Tax and Gift Tax Act; and Art. 74, VAT Act).[19] Pursuant to Article 31 of the Adjustment of International Taxes Act (AITA), the Korean Competent Authority will obtain and exchange information requested by its EOI partner under a DTC, a TIEA, or a multilateral instrument. These very broad powers apply whether the information requested relates to legal and beneficial ownership, accounting, or banking information.

193. In criminal tax matters, NTS officials may question suspects of such offences and have powers to search and seize documents (Art. 2, Procedure for Punishment of Tax Evaders Act). To use these powers, a warrant from a judge of the competent District Court must be obtained.

194. For EOI purposes, the Korean authorities advise that they use the access to information measures granted by the relevant tax acts to answer incoming requests. Considering the wide range of powers to gather information provided by these laws, there has been no need to obtain a warrant from a judge and use a specific search and seizure procedure.

---

19. Financial institutions are covered by the Corporate Tax Act.

Access to ownership, accounting and banking information in practice

195. The Korean Competent Authority is the Minister of Economy and Finance and the Director of the Offshore Compliance Division of the NTS is the authorised representative of the Minister. The Offshore Compliance Division is a central office located in Sejong and is responsible for all international EOI activities.

196. As described above, the Competent Authority has broad powers to obtain all types of relevant information including legal and beneficial ownership, accounting and banking information from any person. The 2012 Report (paragraph 236) described the IT system used by the NTS at the time. This system was replaced in 2015 by the NTS system, which contains the same information as the previous IT system. The NTS system is available to all NTS officials (although information accessibility restrictions apply). Offshore Compliance Division staff also have access to other government databases, such as information maintained by the Register office, the real estate register, or customs information.

197. In practice, upon receipt of an EOI request, the Offshore Compliance Division uploads the request and supporting documentation to its electronic system (called the Automatic exchange and analysis of foreign financial information system or AXIS system[20]) and then verifies the conformity of the request with tax treaties and domestic laws. If the Offshore Compliance Division cannot obtain the requested information from the NTS system or other government databases, then the Offshore Compliance Division translates the request and forwards it to the appropriate Regional or District Tax Offices using the AXIS system in order to gather the information from the taxpayer or third parties (other than financial institutions). The Director of the relevant Regional or District Tax Office appoints an official to collect the requested information. Once the information is collected, it is uploaded onto the AXIS system and forwarded to the Offshore Compliance Division. The Offshore Compliance Division verifies that the information responds to the EOI request, translates it into English and sends the information to the requesting partner.

198. All requests for banking information are processed by the Offshore Compliance Division. In order to access banking information, the Competent Authority sends a letter to a financial institution requesting for the information to be provided within 30 days, along with a standardised form prescribed by the FSC (Art. 4, Act on Real Name Financial Transactions and Confidentiality). The letter only includes a reference to the domestic legal

---

20. The AXIS system was developed in 2016 which is used by the Offshore Compliance Division to process incoming and outgoing EOI requests. For more information regarding the AXIS system refer to element C.5.

provision under which the information is requested and personal information of the account-holder (including name, TIN, account number, deed number or other information by which the financial institution can identify the transaction information (Art. 10, Enforcement Decree of the Act on Real Name Financial Transactions and Confidentiality). However, if the request relates to a group request or the personal information of the account-holder is not available, then such information need not be provided (Art. 31, AITA and Art. 47, Enforcement Decree of AITA).

199. As confirmed by peer input, there was no case during the review period where Korea failed to obtain ownership, accounting, or banking information for EOI purposes due to an inability to access such information.

B.1.3. Use of information gathering measures absent domestic tax interest

200. The concept of "domestic tax interest" describes a situation where a contracting party can only provide information to another contracting party if it has an interest in the requested information for its own tax purposes.

201. Korea has no domestic tax interest limitation with respect to its information gathering powers pursuant to the AITA.

202. Information gathering powers provided to the NTS under the AITA may be used to respond to EOI requests regardless of whether Korea needs the information for its own domestic tax purposes. Nineteen of the EOI requests received by Korea requested information in which Korea had no domestic tax interest.

B.1.4. Effective enforcement provisions to compel the production of information

203. Korea has in place effective enforcement provisions to compel the production of information. For EOI purposes, pursuant to the AITA, the NTS may exercise its inquiry and investigation powers as provided in respective tax laws to obtain the information, such as by making a request for document submission, conducting an interview and on-site inspections. Also, the NTS may conduct search and seizure with a warrant issued by a judge when the on-site inspection turns into a criminal investigation after the identification of tax evasion charges.

204. Where a financial institution fails to comply or provides false information, a penalty not exceeding KRW 30 million (EUR 22 090) may be imposed (Art. 31-4, AITA). Where a person, other than a financial institution, refuses to comply or makes a false statement to a legitimate inquiry or investigation by the NTS, a penalty of up to KRW 20 million (EUR 14 727) may be imposed (Art. 88, Framework Act on National Taxes).

205. Besides the application of fines, the main consequence, when information is not provided in relation to queries posed, is to assess taxes according to the information already available with the NTS. Failure to provide the requested information may also be taken as grounds for the NTS to launch a tax audit for tax evasion against the person concerned (which may be necessary in order to obtain a warrant for search and seizure).

206. NTS officials indicated that sanctions are rarely used as in almost all cases the persons concerned are co-operative and provide answers in a timely manner. The domestic law does not provide for a timeframe in respect of the response from the information holder; however, the internal policy of the Offshore Compliance Division is that the information holder has 30 days to respond, with one extension period of 30 days. NTS officials advise the extension period may be granted in cases where the request is complex or involves a large volume of data. Where an information holder has not responded within 30 days, and the extension has not been granted, the information holder has failed to complied and may be subject to a penalty of up to KRW 20 million (EUR 14 727).

207. In practice, there were no cases where a person failed to provide information requested during the peer review period and the NTS did not need to seek a warrant to conduct a search and seizure. In cases where a person refuses to co-operate, the NTA confirmed that it would use its compulsory powers to ensure that the requested information is obtained and provided. The NTS would make a request to the prosecutor's office to apply to the court for a warrant. The timeframe to obtain a warrant varies on a case-by-case basis. No concerns in this respect were reported by peers.

B.1.5. Secrecy provisions

208. Although there are a range of confidentiality and secrecy provisions that apply to entities and arrangements in Korea, these provisions are overridden for EOI purposes.

209. The Act on Real Name Financial Transactions and Confidentiality, which prohibits a financial institution from providing information to third parties without prior consent of the account-holder, does not apply to Korea's Competent Authority when accessing information maintained by a financial institution in order to respond to an EOI request, including information pertaining to CDD (Art. 31, AITA).

210. The Attorney at Law Act sets out the attorney-client privilege. The scope of the confidentiality provision is strictly limited to confidential matters that the attorney has learned in the course of performing his/her duties; however this provision does not apply to cases where such disclosure of confidential matters is especially prescribed otherwise by Acts. Where an

attorney acts in any other capacity (e.g. as a real estate broker or in a fiduciary capacity), the attorney client privilege does not apply. The attorney-client privilege in Korea meets the international standard. Refer to paragraphs 263-264 of the 2012 Report for details.

211. Korean law also recognises a protection against disclosure of information by certified judicial scriveners and certified public accountants; however, the secrecy provision contained in the Judicial Scrivener Act and the Certified Public Accountants Act is overridden by Article 31 of the AITA. Accordingly, the confidentiality obligations of judicial scriveners and public accountants, does not prevent the disclosure of information to the NTS. Refer to paragraphs 265-266 of the 2012 Report.

212. In practice, information is routinely obtained from financial institutions, and it has happened that information was asked to a lawyer. There were no cases during the review period where banking secrecy or attorney-client privilege was an impediment to obtaining the requested information. No concerns in this respect were reported by peers.

B.2. Notification requirements, rights and safeguards

> The rights and safeguards (e.g. notification, appeal rights) that apply to persons in the requested jurisdiction should be compatible with effective exchange of information.

213. The 2012 Report concluded that there was no prior notification procedure in Korea; however, time-specific post-exchange notification existed. There have been no changes to these procedures since that report but the EOIR standard was clarified in 2016 to indicate that post-exchange notifications should be compatible with EOI.

214. When information already in possession of the NTS is exchanged, the NTS must inform the person concerned within ten days after the provision of full information to the requesting party (Art. 47(3) of Enforcement Decree to the AITA). This post-exchange notification is not for guaranteeing the taxpayer's right to challenge the provision of the request but for informing of the provision of information to comply with obligations under an international agreement.

215. The 10-day deadline may be extended up to six months if requested by the requesting partner (Art. 47(4) of Enforcement Decree to the AITA). The deferral of the notification may be requested if: (i) the notification is likely to jeopardise a person's life or body; (ii) the notification is likely to obstruct the fair progress of judicial proceedings, such as the destruction of evidence or a threat to a witness; or (iii) the notification is likely to obstruct

or excessively delay the progress of administrative procedures, such as an inquiry or examination. After the lapse of this period, the notification must be carried out.

216. The 2016 ToR requires that jurisdictions should provide for exceptions from time-specific post-exchange requirement. In Korea, notification may be delayed upon request by the requesting jurisdiction for up to six months from the provision of full information. Although it is acknowledged that after lapse of this period the notification must be carried out, the length of the delay period appears to ensure that the notification is not likely to undermine the change of success of the investigation in the requesting jurisdiction. During the review period, Korea received five requests from one of its major EOI partners to defer notification and accepted all of the requests. No concerns in this respect were raised by peers. The time-specific post-exchange requirement is therefore in line with the standard.

217. In practice, when receiving an EOI request, Korea informs the requesting partner, by email, that notification may be deferred and requests feedback from the partner.

218. Taxpayers have no special rights to intervene against the tax authorities' information-gathering powers, nor do they have any appeals rights.

219. The NTS authorities have indicated that, to date, there have been no cases where taxpayers or third party record keepers refused to provide requested information in response to the tax authorities' information-gathering powers.

220. The table of recommendations, determination and rating is as follows:

Legal and Regulatory Framework
Determination: The element is in place
Practical Implementation of the standard
Rating: Compliant

Part C: Exchanging information

221. Sections C.1 to C.5 evaluate the effectiveness of Korea's network of EOI mechanisms – whether these EOI mechanisms provide for exchange of the right scope of information, cover all Korea's relevant partners, whether there were adequate provisions to ensure the confidentiality of information received, whether Korea's network of EOI mechanisms respects the rights and safeguards of taxpayers and whether Korea can provide the information requested in an effective manner.

C.1. Exchange of information mechanisms

> Exchange of information mechanisms should provide for effective exchange of information.

222. The 2012 Report concluded that Korea's network of EOI mechanisms was in line with the standard and provided for effective EOI. At January 2012, Korea's EOI network covered 86 jurisdictions and Korea had signed, but not yet ratified, the multilateral Convention. Since then, the multilateral Convention entered into force in Korea on 1 July 2012 and Korea's EOI network covers 158 jurisdictions, with 23 new bilateral instruments (8 TIEAs and 15 DTCs) and 7 protocols.

223. No issue in respect of the interpretation of foreseeable relevance was identified in the 2012 Report. In the current review period, all peers providing input, except for one, were satisfied with Korea's interpretation of the foreseeable relevance standard.

224. The table of recommendations, determination and rating is as follows:

Legal and Regulatory Framework
Determination: The element is in place

Practical Implementation of the standard		
	Underlying Factor	**Recommendations**
Deficiencies identified	Korea had problems communicating with one EOI partner regarding the interpretation of the foreseeable relevance standard in 3.5% requests received during the review period.	Korea is recommended to continue clearly communicating with all of its EOI partners to ensure that its interpretation of the foreseeable relevance standard is consistent with Article 26(1) of the OECD Model Convention.
Rating: Compliant		

C.1.1. Foreseeably relevant standard

225. Exchange of information mechanisms should allow for EOIR where it is foreseeably relevant to the administration and enforcement of the domestic tax laws of the requesting jurisdiction. This concept, as articulated in Article 26 of the OECD Model Tax Convention, is to be interpreted broadly, but does not extend as to allow for "fishing expeditions". The Article 26 commentary recognises that the standard of "foreseeable relevance" can be met when alternative terms are used in an agreement, such as "necessary" or "relevant".

226. The 2012 Report concluded that all but four of Korea's agreements met the "foreseeably relevant" standard. The bilateral agreements with Austria and Brazil only allow exchanges for the application of the Convention. The DTC with the Netherlands provides for exchange of "such information (being information which such authorities have in proper order at their disposal) as is necessary…" The DTC with Switzerland required the provision of certain identification information on the person under investigation when making a request. However, the Report noted that as Korea, Brazil and the Netherlands were signatory to the multilateral Convention, EOI to the standard would take place with these jurisdictions once the Convention came into effect in Korea. Further, Korea, Austria and Switzerland were in the process of renegotiating their agreements.

227. Since the 2012 Report, Switzerland and Korea signed a protocol which meets the foreseeably relevant standard. The EOI agreement with Austria has not been renegotiated; however, given that Austria is party to the multilateral Convention, it is in a position to exchange information under the Convention in accordance with the standard. All EOI agreements signed since the 2012 Report are in line with the standard.

228. The Korean Competent Authority reported that it interprets and applies its EOI agreements consistently with the standard of foreseeable

relevance. Also, all incoming EOI requests are processed according to the guidelines set out in their EOI Manual which is based on the EOI Working Manual published by the Global Forum.

229. Korea does not require its EOI partners to complete a standardised template for the formulation of requests and instead receives and accepts requests in a wide variety of formats. If Korea receives a request and it is unclear whether the foreseeable relevance standard has been met, Korea will request additional information or clarifications from the requesting jurisdiction.

230. Concerning the practical application of the criteria of foreseeable relevance, the 2012 Report did not identify any issue. All peers that provided input for this report, except one, confirmed that Korea properly applied the foreseeable relevance standard during the current period under review.

231. Korea challenged the foreseeable relevance in 22 cases (of which 11 concerned the requests made by one peer) and asked for clarification on issues other than foreseeable relevance in 5 cases. Once partners responded with the clarification, Korea provided the requested information to 15 of the 27 requests, declined to provide the information to 11 requests and considered 1 request to be withdrawn.

232. The partner that sent the 11 requests (all relating to transfer pricing issues) expressed concerns that Korea's threshold for demonstrating foreseeable relevance was too restrictive. These requests were sent to Korea between 2016 and 2018. Korea sent letters declining ten of these requests, without consulting the partner, based on, in some cases, a restrictive interpretation of foreseeable relevance.[21] With respect to the eleventh request, Korea sent a letter seeking clarification in order to establish foreseeable relevance. The partner responded to four of the letters declining the requests in 2016; however, Korea did not further communicate with this partner on these requests. The partner did not respond to the other six letters and one clarification request. The partner advised that the reasons for declining the requests were identical to the other four requests and the issue was already clarified. The partner had to close all the cases due to the statute of limitation without the information requested from Korea.

233. This gives rise to two issues, first, declining a request without consulting the requesting jurisdiction (see discussion under C.5.1) and second, the interpretation of foreseeable relevance. As mentioned in the Commentary on Article 26 of the Model Tax Convention, "the standard of foreseeable relevance is intended to provide for exchange of information in tax matters to the widest possible extent". The assessment team reviewed anonymised versions of the requests, Korea's correspondence and the partner's responses

---

21. These represent 3.5% of the total EOI requests received during the review period.

thereto and found that Korea's interpretation of the standard may have been too restrictive at times. Although no other peers raised any concerns with respect to Korea's interpretation of foreseeable relevance, it is recommended that Korea monitor its interpretation of the foreseeable relevance standard to ensure that it is consistent with Article 26(1) of the OECD Model Convention in all cases.

Group requests

234. Korea's EOI agreements and domestic law do not contain language prohibiting group requests. Korea interprets them as allowing providing information requested pursuant to group requests in line with Article 26 of the OECD Model Tax Convention and its commentaries. The basic process and procedures for responding to group requests follows those applicable to ordinary, non-group requests.

235. During the period under review Korea received one group request; however, the request was validly declined as it was not signed by the appropriate Competent Authority. The Korean authorities confirmed that they would answer a group request, if the information provided mirrors the information required to be provided in Paragraph 5.2 of the Commentary to Article 26 of the 2012 Update to the OECD Model Tax Convention.

C.1.2. Provide for exchange of information in respect of all persons

236. Korea's EOI agreements provide for EOI in respect to all persons. During the review period, Korea received 19 requests related to persons who were not taxpayers in Korea and there was no domestic tax interest in obtaining the requested information. Korea was able to provide the requested information.

C.1.3. Obligation to exchange all types of information and C.1.4. Absence of domestic tax interest

237. The OECD Model Tax Convention Article 26(5) and the Model TIEA Article 5(4), which are authoritative sources of the standard, stipulate that bank secrecy cannot form the basis for declining a request to provide information and that a request for information cannot be declined solely because the information is held by nominees or persons acting in an agency or fiduciary capacity or because the information relates to an ownership interest.

238. In terms of domestic interest restrictions, contracting parties must use their information gathering measures even though invoked solely to obtain and provide information to the other contracting party. Such obligation

is explicitly contained in the OECD Model Tax Convention Article 26(4) and Article 5(2) of the Model TIEA.

239. The 2012 Report concluded that Korea's DTCs with Austria, Luxembourg, the Netherlands and Malaysia did not comply with the international standard; however, at that time, protocols updating the DTC with the Netherlands had been signed, while the protocols updating the DTCs with Austria, Luxembourg and Malaysia had been initialled.[22] Also, Korea and the Netherlands were signatories to the multilateral Convention. The report further found that although most of Korea's EOI agreements did not contain a provision equivalent to Article 26(5) of the Model Tax Convention, there were no restrictions in the Korean authorities' capacity to access banking information, therefore the agreements complied with the international standard. Restrictions in access to banking information may however exist for some of Korea's treaty partners, therefore an in-text recommendation in the 2012 Report was included for Korea to continue to monitor effective EOI between such partners and, if necessary, renegotiate its older DTCs.

240. The 2012 Report concluded also that, with the exception of five DTCs, three protocols and three TIEAs, Korea's EOI agreements did not contain wording akin to Article 26(4) of the Model Tax Convention. Nevertheless, there were no domestic interest restrictions on Korea's powers to access information. The report concluded that a domestic tax interest requirement may, however, exist for some of Korea's treaty partners. As such, an in-text recommendation was included for Korea to continue to monitor effective EOI between such partners and, if necessary, renegotiate its older DTCs.

241. Since that report, the multilateral Convention entered into force in Korea, protocols with seven partners have entered into force and four new DTCs with existing EOI partners have been signed (with one ratified), which allow Korea and these partners to exchange information in accordance with the standard.[23] Further, the EOI agreements entered into since the 2012 Report allow information to be obtained and exchanged even if it is not required for domestic tax purposes.

---

22. There has been no change to the status of the protocols with Austria, the Netherlands and Malaysia since the 2012 Report as the authorities from these jurisdictions and Korea agreed not to proceed with the protocols because these jurisdictions would become parties to the Multilateral Convention.
23. These were the protocols with Belgium, Brazil, Italy, Luxembourg, Poland, Singapore and Switzerland, and the DTCs with Czech Republic, India, Singapore and the United Arab Emirates.

242. Out of Korea's DTCs, 72 do not contain Articles 26(4) or 26(5) of the Model Tax Convention.[24] Fifty-two of these partner jurisdictions are signatories to the multilateral Convention, therefore Korea is able to exchange information in line with the standard with them on this basis. The remaining jurisdictions have not (yet) been reviewed by the Global Forum and may have restrictions which may limit effective EOI under the respective DTCs.[25] However, Korea has contacted each of these jurisdictions, proposing to amend the existing DTC to align it with the standard, but, to date, Korea has not received answers to these proposals.

243. In practice, there have been no cases where the requested information was not provided because it was held by a bank, another financial institution, a nominee or person acting in an agency or a fiduciary capacity, or because it related to ownership interests in a person when applying a DTC that does not contain an explicit provision in this regard. In particular, during the period under review, Korea dealt with 77 requests for banking information (refer to sections B.1 and C.5). There have also been no issues linked to domestic tax interest and this is confirmed by peers.

C.1.5. Absence of dual criminality principles and C.1.6. Exchange information relating to both civil and criminal tax matters

244. All of Korea's EOI agreements provide for EOI in both civil and criminal matters. None of Korea's EOI agreements contain restrictions limiting EOI in criminal matters or based on dual criminality principles. Korea answered all requests during the review period, whether they related to civil or criminal tax matters. Peers did not raise any issues.

---

24. Albania, Algeria, Australia, Austria, Azerbaijan, Bangladesh, Belarus, Belgium, Bulgaria, Chile, China (People's Republic of), Croatia, Czech Republic, Denmark, Egypt, Estonia, Ethiopia, Fiji, Finland, Georgia, Germany, Greece, Hungary, Iceland, Indonesia, Iran, Ireland, Israel, Japan, Jordan, Kazakhstan, Kuwait, Kyrgyzstan, Lao People's Democratic Republic, Latvia, Lithuania, Malaysia, Malta, Mexico, Mongolia, Morocco, Myanmar, Nepal, Netherlands, Nigeria, Norway, Oman, Pakistan, Papua New Guinea, Philippines, Portugal, Qatar, Romania, Russia, Saudi Arabia, Slovak Republic, Slovenia, South Africa, Spain, Sri Lanka, Sudan, Sweden, Thailand, Tunisia, Turkey, Ukraine, United Arab Emirates, United Kingdom, United States, Uzbekistan, Venezuela and Viet Nam.
25. These are Algeria, Bangladesh, Belarus, Egypt, Ethiopia, Fiji, Iran, Jordan, Kyrgyzstan, Lao People's Democratic Republic, Myanmar, Nepal, Nigeria, Papua New Guinea, Sri Lanka, Sudan, Thailand, Uzbekistan, Venezuela and Viet Nam.

C.1.7. Provide information in specific form requested

245. There are no restrictions in Korea's EOI agreements that would prevent it from providing information in a specific form, as long as this is consistent with its own administrative practices. No peers raised any concerns.

C.1.8. Signed agreements should be in force and
C.1.9. Be given effect through domestic law

246. At the time of the 2012 Report, Korea's EOI network covered 86 partners. Of the EOI agreements signed, three TIEAs, five DTCs and three protocols were not yet in force.[26] Generally, EOI agreements signed by Korea were ratified by both parties within 18 months of their signature, although there were four instances where entry into force was delayed. However, in most instances Korea had taken all steps necessary to bring into force these four EOI agreements.

247. Since then, all of these EOI agreements have entered into force, with the exception of the DTCs with Sudan and Nigeria. The multilateral Convention entered into force in Korea on 1 July 2012. Further, Korea has signed 8 TIEAs, 15 DTCs, and 4 protocols since the 2012 Report, and all are in force except for 2 DTCs. Korea has ratified the DTC with the United Arab Emirates and ratification is pending on the other side. The DTC with Cambodia was recently signed and Korea is taking steps to ratify it. Korea's EOI network now covers 158 jurisdictions through 108 bilateral agreements and the multilateral Convention.

248. The following table summarises the outcomes of the analysis under element C.1 in respect of Korea's EOI relationships:

Total EOI relationships, **including** bilateral and multilateral or regional mechanisms	158
In force	142
In line with the standard	142
Not in line with the standard	0
Signed but not in force	16
In line with the standard	16[a]
Not in line with the standard	0

---

26. These were the TIEAs with the Bahamas, the Cook Islands and the Marshall Islands, the DTCs with Colombia, Gabon, Panama, Sudan and Uruguay, and the protocols with Belgium, Singapore and Switzerland.

Among which – Bilateral mechanisms (DTCs/TIEAs) **not complemented** by multilateral or regional mechanisms	23
In force	**20**
In line with the standard	20
Not in line with the standard	0
Signed but not in force	**3**
In line with the standard	1
Not in line with the standard	2[b]

Notes: a. The multilateral Convention is currently not in force in these jurisdictions: Armenia (enters into force on 1 June 2020), Benin, Bosnia and Herzegovina, Burkina Faso, Cabo Verde (enters into force on 1 May 2020), Gabon, Kenya, Liberia, Mauritania, Mongolia (enters into force of 1 June 2020), Montenegro (enters into force on 1 May 2020), Oman, Paraguay, Philippines, Togo and United States.

b. These are the agreements with Nigeria and Sudan, see paragraph 242.

249. For EOI to be effective, the parties to an EOI agreement must enact any legislation necessary to comply with the terms of the agreement. Korea has in place the legal and regulatory framework to give effect to its EOI agreements.

250. Effective implementation of EOI agreements in domestic law has been confirmed in practice as there was no case encountered where Korea was not able to obtain and provide the requested information due to unclear or limited effect of an EOI agreement in Korea's law.

C.2. Exchange of information mechanisms with all relevant partners

> The jurisdiction's network of information exchange mechanisms should cover all relevant partners.

251. The 2012 Report did not identify any issue in respect of the scope of Korea's EOI network or its negotiation policy. It was recommended that Korea continue to develop its EOI network with all relevant partners.

252. Since that report, Korea has expanded its EOI network from 86 to 158 jurisdictions, through of 96 DTCs, 12 TIEAs and the multilateral Convention. Korea's EOI network encompasses a wide range of counterparties, including all its major trading partners, all the G20 members and all OECD members. No peer advised that Korea had refused to negotiate or sign an EOI agreement with it.

253. As the standard ultimately requires that jurisdictions establish an EOI relationship up to the standard with all partners who are interested in entering into such a relationship Korea should continue to conclude EOI agreements with any new relevant partner who would so require (refer to Annex 1).

254. The table of recommendations, determination and rating is as follows:

Legal and Regulatory Framework
Determination: The element is in place
Practical Implementation of the standard
Rating: Compliant

C.3. Confidentiality

> The jurisdiction's information exchange mechanisms should have adequate provisions to ensure the confidentiality of information received.

255. The applicable EOI agreement provisions and domestic laws that apply to officials with access to EOI information and the practice in Korea regarding confidentiality are in accordance with the standard. There are adequate confidentiality provisions protecting tax information under Korea's domestic laws. No case of breach of confidentiality has been encountered in the EOI context and no concerns have been reported by peers.

256. The table of recommendations, determination and rating is as follows:

Legal and Regulatory Framework
Determination: The element is in place
Practical Implementation of the standard
Rating: Compliant

C.3.1. Information received: disclosure, use and safeguards

257. The 2012 Report concluded that all of Korea's EOI agreements meet the standard for confidentiality including the limitations on disclosure of information received and use of the information exchanged, which are reflected in Article 26(2) of the OECD Model Tax Convention and Article 8 of the OECD Model TIEA. The EOI agreements that Korea has signed since that report all contain confidentiality provisions consistent with the standard.

258. There are adequate confidentiality provisions protecting tax information contained in the Framework Act on National Taxes. When confidential information is disclosed, Article 127 of the Criminal Act provides that the official in breach of confidentiality may be subject to imprisonment of up to two years or a suspension of qualifications[27] up to five years. There has been no change in these provisions since the 2012 Report.

---

27. Suspension of qualifications under the Criminal Act means that an individual is disqualified from: (i) becoming a public official; (ii) voting rights and eligibility

259. The NTS conducts background checks and screenings for tax officials and contractors based on the procedures described in NTS Security Operation Regulation. All tax officials are required to sign a confidentiality agreement when they first begin employment and every six months thereafter. Where the NTS enters into any contract with an outside service provider, a non-disclosure agreement is made between the NTS and the contractor. The representative and employees of the third-party contractor submit a written pledge of confidentiality to the NTS. These confidentiality obligations apply for the duration of employment (or contract) and remain applicable after employment (or contract) ends.

260. The NTS provides training to employees and contractors regarding confidential information. The NTS requires on-the-job training courses run by the NTS Information Security Officials, for the newly employed, including contract workers. As part of periodic security awareness training, a weekly email regarding information security issues and tips is sent by the security audit division of the information protection team at the NTS to NTS employees and contractors to raise awareness of information security. Further, at least twice a year, managers of a team or division are required to provide information security training to his/her team members. In addition, officials responsible for information security at the NTS and regional tax offices visit district tax offices to provide training regarding information security updates once a year. A "clean screen and desktop" policy also applies within the NTS.

261. EOI-related tasks are centralised within the Offshore Compliance Division of the NTS. Offshore Compliance Division staff have also received specific training on handling EOI matters and the NTS has adopted an EOI Manual which sets out the procedures and obligations related to confidentiality. All hard copy information received concerning an EOI request are kept in folders that are locked in secure filing cabinets in the Offshore Compliance Division office (and is separate from domestic tax information). All information received related to EOI is scanned onto the AXIS system. The AXIS system is on a secure server and accessible only to Offshore Compliance Division staff and authorised NTS officials.

262. All translation of incoming or outgoing requests, as well as information relevant to an EOI request, is done by an Offshore Compliance Division staff to avoid any disclosure of information. Disclosure of EOI information outside of the Offshore Compliance Division, whether to another government agency or to a third party, contains reference to the Korean domestic law pursuant to which the information is requested and a description of the information requested.

---

to run in public elections; and (iii) qualifying to conduct certain business/professions prescribed by Acts (such as acting as a lawyer or accountant).

263. A Korean taxpayer is allowed to inspect or obtain a copy of the determination note that includes the underlying facts and grounds of taxation. The taxpayer subject to an EOI request or the information holder are not in a position to request inspection of the EOI request as it is not part of the basis of a determination note in Korea. Further, the taxpayers' files do not include EOI requests as these are kept centrally in the Competent Authority's archive accessible only by EOI officials on a need to know basis.

264. The NTS has manned security as well as automatic access controls in its premises. Employees have been issued ID cards which are recognised at the gates for entry and exit accesses. Their entry and exit are monitored and logged. All NTS premises have restricted access and all visitors are screened before admittance, including showing a valid ID. Access to the Offshore Compliance Division office is limited to authorised officials and is controlled by a security system.

265. Korea treats all information related to an EOI request as confidential and will use the information only for tax purposes unless otherwise agreed between Korea and its EOI partner. There were no cases during the review period where the information received from an EOI partner was used by Korea for purposes other than tax and Korea did not receive any requests from its partners to approve the non-tax use of information exchanged.

266. No case of breach of the confidentiality obligation in respect of EOI has been encountered by the Korean authorities and no peers raised any concerns.

C.3.2. Confidentiality of other information

267. Korean authorities confirm that confidentiality rules apply to all types of information exchanged, including information provided by a requesting jurisdiction in a request, information transmitted in response to a request and any background documents to such request.

C.4. Rights and safeguards of taxpayers and third parties

> The information exchange mechanisms should respect the rights and safeguards of taxpayers and third parties.

268. The international standard allows requested parties to not supply information in response to a request in certain identified situations where an issue of trade, business or other secret may arise. Among other reasons, an information request can be declined where the requested information would disclose confidential communications protected by the attorney-client privilege.

269. All of Korea's EOI agreements incorporate wording modelled on Article 26(2) of the Model Tax Convention or Article 8 of the Model TIEA.

270. There was no instance during the previous or current review period where a person refused to provide the requested information because of professional secrecy. Further, Korea did not decline to provide the requested information because it was covered by legal professional privilege or any other professional secret. No peer indicated any issue in this respect.

271. The table of recommendations, determination and rating is as follows:

Legal and Regulatory Framework
Determination: The element is in place
Practical Implementation of the standard
Rating: Compliant

C.5. Requesting and providing information in an effective manner

> The jurisdiction should request and provide information under its network of agreements in an effective manner.

272. The 2012 Report assessed Korea's EOIR practice from 2008 to 2010, during which it had received 166 requests from 28 partners and concluded that Korea had adequate organisational structures and resources to handle incoming EOI requests and provided information in an effective manner. Peers were satisfied with their EOI relationship with Korea and reported a high quality of responses, although sometimes with delays. The report noted that at the end of the review period Korea had implemented new policies which significantly improved its EOI practices.

273. Since that report, Korea implemented a new computerised system to improve the management of EOI information (i.e. the AXIS system). This system has led to improved response times and the provision of status updates during the current review period (2016 to 2018).

274. All 22 peers that provided input, except one, expressed their satisfaction with Korea's quality of incoming and outgoing EOI requests and the timeliness of responses. Peers were also satisfied with the quality of communication with Korea's EOI unit. Peers did note that status updates, particularly at the beginning of the review period, were not provided; however, there was noticeable improvement in the last year of the review period.

275. The table of recommendations, determination and rating is as follows:

Legal and Regulatory Framework		
This element involves issues of practice. Accordingly, no determination has been made.		
Practical Implementation of the standard		
	Underlying Factor	Recommendations
Deficiencies identified	Korea did not provide any status updates in the first year of the review period. Korea introduced updates to its computer system which increased the number of status updates being provided in the last year of the review period to 65%.	Korea is recommended to continue to ensure that it provides status updates in all cases where it takes over 90 days to provide a response.
Rating: Compliant		

C.5.1. Timeliness of responses to requests for information

276. Over the period under review (1 January 2016 to 31 December 2018), Korea received a total of 289 requests for information from 31 EOI partners. Japan is by far Korea's main EOI partner representing 42% of Korea's incoming requests. The information requested related to (i) ownership and identity information (21 cases), (ii) accounting information (126 cases), (iii) banking information (77 cases) and (iv) other types of information (260 cases). The legal entities and arrangements for which information was requested are broken down to companies (158 cases) and trusts (1 case).[28]

277. The following table relates to the requests received during the period under review and gives an overview of response times needed by Korea to provide a final response to these requests, together with a summary of other relevant factors impacting the effectiveness of Korea's EOI practice during the reviewed period.

---

28. Please note that some requests entailed more than one information category and/or more than one individual or entity type.

Statistics on response time

		2016		2017		2018		Total	
		Num.	%	Num.	%	Num.	%	Num.	%
Total number of requests received	[A+B+C+D+E+F:G]	96	100	104	100	89	100	289	100
Full response: ≤90 days		35	36	26	25	49	55	110	38
≤ 180 days (cumulative)		70	73	66	63	75	84	211	73
≤ 1 year (cumulative)	[A]	78	81	90	87	86	97	254	88
> 1 year	[B]	9	9	12	12	0	0	21	7
Declined for valid reasons	[C]	0	0	0	0	1	1	1	1
Status update provided within 90 days (for outstanding cases with full information not provided within 90 days, responses provided > 90 days)		0	0	9	12	24	65	33	20
Requests withdrawn by requesting jurisdiction	[D]	0	0	0	0	2	2	2	0.7
Requests considered by Korea as withdrawn by requesting jurisdiction	[E]	0	0	1	0.9	0	0	1	0.3
Failure to obtain and provide information requested	[F]	9	9	1	0.9	0	0	10	3
Requests still pending at date of review	[G]	0	0	0	0	0	0	0	0

Notes: a. Requests are counted as per the number of taxpayers subject of the request. If a request relates to one taxpayer, it is counted as one even where more than one piece of information is requested. If Korea received a further request for information that relates to a pervious request, with the original request still active, Korea will append the additional request to the original and continue to count it as the same request.

b. The time periods in this table are counted from the date of receipt of the request to the date on which the final and complete response was issued.

278. Although the average time of responses within 90 days remains relatively low at 38%, this has improved over the current three-year review period (from 36% to 55%). The requests that Korea was able to respond to within 90 days were requests where: the information was available with the NTS, other government agencies or banks; the requests were simple; or the information holder provided the information within 30 days and did not request an extension.

279. The average time it took Korea to respond to requests within 180 days and within one year was 73% and 88% respectively. There was noticeable improvement in these statistics over the current three-year review period. In 2018, Korea responded to 84% of requests within 180 days and 97% of requests within a year.

280. The timeliness statistics from this current review period compared to those in the 2012 Report are comparable even though Korea receive almost double the number of incoming requests this review period (from 166 to 289 requests).

281. According to Korean officials the reasons why it may have taken longer than 180 days to respond to EOI requests: (i) some requests were

complicated and required the information holder(s) be interviewed; (ii) the number of questions or requested information contained in a single request may have been numerous, for instance in one request the EOI partner sought information with respect to 52 entities; (iii) requests related to transfer pricing issues are relatively complex and require a longer period of time for the company(ies) to collect the requested information; (iv) companies subject of the requests were in the middle of legal proceedings and Korea had to inform its EOI partners that it needed additional time to collect the information from those companies once the proceedings had been completed; and (v) some requests requested hard-copies of documents that were older than the retention period requirements, which required the information holder to seek the documents from their archives.

282. Korean officials explained that the main reason that some requests took longer than a year to process is due to its EOI partners taking a long time to answer the requests for clarification. During the period under review, Korea requested clarifications in 27 cases representing 9% of the total cases from the requesting partners. The NTS confirms that these clarifications were sought only when it was necessary to verify the foreseeably relevance or when deemed necessary for correctly understanding the details of the request and collecting accurate information as quickly as possible. Only one peer raised concerns regarding Korea's requests for clarification and interpretation of the foreseeable relevance standard (refer to section C.1.1 above).

283. NTS officials indicated that its response times improved from 2016 to 2018 due to: the implementation of the new computerised AXIS system; improved EOI procedure to gather information; training and awareness-building activities on EOI to field auditors gathering the information; and a closer monitoring of deadlines by the Offshore Compliance Division. Based on these new measures, NTS officials advise that in 2019 they responded to 66% of requests within 90 days, 96% of requests within 180 days and 99% of requests within a year. Korea should continue to ensure a good level of clear communication with its EOI partners and improve the timeliness of its responses (refer to paragraphs 287 and 296 and Annex I).

284. Out of the 289 EOI requests received during the peer review period, Korea validly declined one request as it was not sent by the appropriate Competent Authority. Before declining a request, the Offshore Compliance Division contacts the requesting partner to request additional information or clarifications as needed. During the review period, two requests were withdrawn. In one case, the EOI partner responded to Korea's request for clarification saying that the tax examination was nearing completion and that the information was no longer needed, and in the other, the partner indicated that the information was no longer necessary as the tax audit had been completed.

285. There are ten requests categorised as failure to obtain and provide the information requested and one request labelled as a request considered by Korea to have been withdrawn. These 11 requests are those discussed in section C.1.1. As explained, ten letters were sent to the partner indicated that Korea was declining the requests, without discussing the issues with the partner (see discussion below). These ten requests have therefore been treated as failures to provide the requested information. As for the remaining request, the partner did not respond to Korea's request for clarification, therefore NTS officials considered that the partner had withdrawn this request. This had an impact for the EOI partner, which had to close the 11 cases without the information requested from Korea.

Status updates and communication with EOI partners

286. During the review period, Korea provided status updates on average in 20% of cases where required under the standard. The percentage of status updates significantly increased over the review period from 0% in the first year to 65% in the last year. According to NTS officials, the improvement of providing status updates is a result of annual updates made to the AXIS system and the upgrade in 2019 to the AXIS system which now has an automatic pop-up reminder of the 90-day deadline which only disappears when a status update email is sent to the requesting partner and the update is uploaded onto the system. The 90-day countdown runs continuously, with a pop-up reminder sent before each 90-day interval, until a request in closed. Status updates are provided by the Offshore Compliance Division officer handling the case typically by email where no protected data are required to be disclosed. According to Korean officials, in 2019 status updates were provided in all cases where required. It is recommended that Korea continue to ensure that it provides status updates in all cases where it takes over 90 days to provide a response.

287. Declining a request before consulting the requesting jurisdiction does not ensure effective exchange of information. Korea maintains that the letters it sent declining the requests were meant to seek clarification. When seeking clarification, the letter should clearly indicate that the requested jurisdiction is seeking clarification. NTS officials are now aware that their requests for clarification must be clear. Nevertheless, Korea should continue to ensure a good level of clear communication with its EOI partners and improve the timeliness of its responses (refer to paragraphs 283 and 296 and Annex 1).

C.5.2. Organisational processes and resources

288. The Competent Authority in Korea is the Minister of Economy and Finance. In practice, this function is delegated to the Director of the Offshore Compliance Division of the NTS. The contact details of the Competent

Authority are found on the Global Forum's secure competent authorities database. Peer input is positive in connection with the ease of contacting the Korean Competent Authority.

289. All matters relating to EOI are carried out by the Offshore Compliance Division. The division is divided into two units: EOI Unit 1 is in charge of AEOI, while EOI Unit 2 handles spontaneous and EOIR. There are 11 officials in this division, the Director of the division, one deputy director in each EOI Unit, three working-level tax officials in each EOI Unit, a computer system manager in EOI Unit 1 and a translator in EOI Unit 2. Offshore Compliance Division officials have attended training courses offered by the NTS, the OECD and the International Bureau of Fiscal Documentation (IBFD) in international taxation, international investigation and collecting and analysing offshore tax evasion.

290. There are also six employees of a third-party contractor that work with the Offshore Compliance Division who are responsible for maintaining the AXIS system. As discussed in element C.3, these employees are subject to confidentiality requirements.

Incoming requests

291. The 2012 Report concluded that Korea's organisational processes and resources in respect of handling incoming requests were in line with the standard. The AXIS system was introduced in March 2016 which changed some of the organisational processes described in the 2012 Report.

292. When receiving EOI requests from an EOI partner, an official from the Offshore Compliance Division will upload the request and supplementary documents onto the AXIS system. The system automatically allocates a management number to the request which allows Offshore Compliance Division officials to easily track the status of each EOI request. The AXIS system is only accessible to Offshore Compliance Division officials and one designated EOI administrator at each Regional or District Tax Office.

293. Once the EOI request is uploaded on to the AXIS system, the official will check its validity using a checklist set out in the EOI Manual. This EOI Manual has been annually updated since 2010, is based on the OECD Manual on Information Exchange and is available to all NTS officials involved in EOI. If any problems are found with the request, the official will contact the EOI partner to clarify the request.

294. If the EOI request is valid and the requested information is available on the NTS system or other government database accessible to the Offshore Compliance Division official, that official will collect the requested information and send this information to the requesting partner. If the request is for

banking information or information held by another government agency, the official will send a request letter to that information holder in order to collect the information.

295. If the requested information is in the possession or control of a taxpayer or third party (other than a financial institution), the request is translated (within the Offshore Compliance Division, which according to EOI officials generally only takes a few hours) and sent to the EOI administrator at the competent Regional or District Tax Office using the AXIS system. The EOI administrator appoints a field officer to collect the information. The NTS will only disclose the domestic legal provision under which the information is requested to the information holder. EOI officers provide guidance to field officers regarding the precautions and procedures of collecting the information and continually monitor the officers through emails or phone calls. Internal policy requires that the information holder be contacted within 15 days and the information holder has 30 days to respond. A penalty of up to KRW 20 million (EUR 14 727) may be imposed on an information holder who fails to comply or makes a false statement in response to the NTS inquiry. Information collected by the Regional or District Tax Office must be uploaded onto the AXIS system within 7 days and the Offshore Compliance Division is notified. The Offshore Compliance Division official will verify that the information responds to the EOI request (if it does not then the Regional or District Tax Office is contacted and asked to collect the appropriate information). The information, other than supporting documentation, is then translated (which according to EOI officials generally only takes a few hours) and sent to the requesting partner.

296. In practice, Korea generally waits until it has a full response to an EOI request before sending the information to its partner. Usually this is because all of the requested information comes from one information holder. When there are multiple information holders, partial responses may be sent as the information is received by the NTS. According to NTS officials, there were only eight cases during the review period where partial information was sent. No changes have been made to this practice as a result of the new EOI policies. This practice may have implications for a requesting jurisdiction's ability to continue its domestic investigation and on the timeliness of Korea providing responses to its EOI partners. Korea should continue to ensure a good level of clear communication with its EOI partners and improve the timeliness of its responses (refer to paragraphs 283 and 287 and Annex 1).

Outgoing requests

297. The EOIR standard was strengthened in 2016 and now addresses the quality of requests made by the assessed jurisdiction. Jurisdictions should have in place organisational processes and resources to ensure the quality of outgoing EOI requests.

298. Korea has experience with requesting information pursuant to EOI and has developed a robust EOI programme for that purpose. During the review period, Korea sent 309 requests for information. The number of requests is counted by the number of request letters (refer to the note under the C.5 statistical table for details). All the peers that provided peer input were generally satisfied with the quality of EOI requests sent by Korea and by the general communication with Korea.

299. The EOI Manual sets out the procedure to follow to prepare and send an EOI request (including group requests). In an investigation or an audit by a Regional or District Tax Office, if it becomes necessary to make an EOI request, the EOI administrator of that office will upload an EOI request form and relevant attachments onto the AXIS system, which is transmitted to the Offshore Compliance Division. The Offshore Compliance Division will review the form and attachments to determine whether the request meets the provisions of the applicable EOI agreement (i.e. the type of tax and the requested period), the foreseeable relevance standard and whether the investigation team has pursued all means available to obtain the information under domestic law. If the request meets these requirements, then the form and the attachments are translated into English and sent to the requested partner. If, however, the request does not meet the requirements, the Offshore Compliance Division will notify the EOI administration of the tax office of that fact through the AXIS system. Information provided by the requested partner is received by the Offshore Compliance Division which will verify and translate the received information. The information is uploaded onto the AXIS system and transmitted to the tax office in charge of the tax examination that requested the information. The EOI officers provide guidance to field officers regarding the precautions and procedures of using the received information and these field officers are continually monitored by EOI officials through emails or phone calls.

Requests for clarification

300. Korea sent 309 EOI requests during the review period and received 18 requests for clarification, representing 6% of the total number of EOI requests set out below.

	2016	2017	2018	Total
Number of EOI requests sent	66	68	175	309
Number of requests for clarification received	0	2	16	18
Number of acknowledgment of receipt for clarification sent	0	2	15	17

301. Korean authorities explained that they typically received requests for clarification because the investigations were complex and involved many

taxpayers. Korea also received a number of requests for clarification to establish the foreseeable relevance of the request. According to some of the peers that sought such clarification, Korea's EOI requests were missing information (such as the years for which the information was being sought or whether there were reasons for not notifying the taxpayer under examination or investigation). In order to ensure that future outgoing requests contain all necessary information to meet the foreseeable relevance standard, the EOI Manual was updated in 2019. Korea should continue to ensure that its outgoing EOI requests are thoroughly prepared (refer to Annex 1).

302. Upon receiving the request for clarification, the request is translated and uploaded onto the AXIS system by the Offshore Compliance Division. The tax office that made the EOI request is notified of the request for clarification through the AXIS system and by email. Although there are no specific rules regarding timeliness, in practice the average time to reply to a request for clarification was 30 days during the review period. Peers indicated that the requests for clarification did not cause any delays.

Communication

303. Korea accepts requests in English. If the request is not in English, the requesting partner will be asked to translate the request. Korea sends outgoing requests in English as agreed with the particular treaty partner.

304. Communication between the Offshore Compliance Division and other NTS offices is conducted through the AXIS system, telephone, or in person to facilitate the processing of EOI requests. Where it is necessary to contact another government agency or financial institution, an official letter, signed by the Director of the Offshore Compliance Division, is sent. Where it is necessary to contact the person or entity subject of the request, or a third party service provider, the Offshore Compliance Division instructs the EOI administration of the Regional or District Tax Office having jurisdiction over that person, entity, or third party to collect the information.

305. External communication with other jurisdictions is done mostly through post courier such as express mail service which provides tracking information. In some cases, Korea will send information through password protected email. E-mails are generally used for sending acknowledgment letters, requests for clarification, or to provide status updates.

C.5.3. Unreasonable, disproportionate or unduly restrictive conditions for EOI

306. There are no factors or issues identified under this element that could unreasonably, disproportionately or unduly restrict effective EOI in Korea.

Annex 1: List of in-text recommendations

The Global Forum may identify issues that have not had and are unlikely in the current circumstances to have more than a negligible impact on EOIR in practice. Nevertheless, there may be a concern that the circumstances may change and the relevance of the issue may increase. In these cases, a recommendation may be made; however, such recommendations should not be placed in the same box as more substantive recommendations. Rather, these recommendations can be mentioned in the text of the report. A list of such recommendations is reproduced below for convenience.

- **Elements A.1 and A.3**: Korea should clarify the terms "if the institution cannot verify the identity of a person" to ensure that financial institutions apply the procedures for identifying and verifying the actual owner(s) of a company in line with the standard (paragraphs 52 and 173).

- **Elements A.1 and A.3**: Since Korean financial institutions conduct ongoing CDD following a risk-based approach, the beneficial ownership information may not be up to date at all times. Although the NTS will have a significant amount of information relevant for identifying beneficial owners, Korea should take measures to ensure that available beneficial ownership information is kept up to date at all times (paragraphs 57 and 176).

- **Element A.2:** As the Trust Act and the Enforcement Decree are not explicitly clear regarding the obligation to maintain underlying documentation, Korea should ensure that underlying documentation, as required under the standard, is being maintained (paragraph 156).

- **Element A.2**: The requirement for trustees to maintain accounting records for personal trusts is a relatively new requirement and although there may be very few personal trusts (domestic and foreign) currently being managed in Korea, this number may increase in the future, Korea should therefore monitor the compliance of trustees to maintain accounting records and underlying documentation (paragraph 161).

- **Element C.2**: Korea should continue to develop its EOI network with all relevant partners (paragraph 253).

- **Element C.5.1**: Korea should continue to ensure a good level of clear communication with its EOI partners and improve the timeliness of its responses (paragraphs 283, 287 and 296).

- **Element C.5.2**: Korea should continue to ensure that its outgoing EOI requests are thoroughly prepared (paragraph 301).

Annex 2: List of Korea's EOI mechanisms

Bilateral international agreements for the exchange of information

	EOI partner	Type of agreement	Signature	Entry into force
1	Albania	DTC	17-May-2006	13-Jan-2007
2	Algeria	DTC	24-Nov-2001	31-Aug-2006
3	Andorra	TIEA	23-Oct-2014	21-Dec-2016
4	Australia	DTC	12-Jul-1982	01-Jan-1984
5	Austria	DTC	08-Oct-1985	01-Dec-1987
6	Azerbaijan	DTC	19-May-2008	25-Nov-2008
7	Bahamas	TIEA	04-Aug-2011	15-Jul-2013
8	Bahrain	DTC	01-May-2012	26-Apr-2013
9	Bangladesh	DTC	10-May-1983	22-Oct-1984
10	Belarus	DTC	20-May-2002	17-Jun-2003
11	Belgium	DTC	29-Aug-1977	19-Sept-1979
11	Belgium	DTC (Protocol)	08-Mar-2010	01-Dec-2015
12	Bermuda	TIEA	23-Jan-2012	13-Feb-2015
13	Brazil	DTC	07-Mar-1989	27-Nov-1991
13	Brazil	DTC (Protocol)	24-Apr-2015	10-Jan-2018
14	British Virgin Islands	TIEA	05-Dec-2014	05-Dec-2016
15	Brunei Darussalam	DTC	09-Dec-2014	14-Oct-2016
16	Bulgaria	DTC	11-Mar-1994	22-Jun-1995
17	Cambodia	DTC	25-Nov-2019	Not ratified by Korea
18	Canada	DTC	05-Sep-2006	18-Dec-2006
19	Chile	DTC	18-Apr-2002	22-Jul-2003
20	China (People's Republic of)	DTC	28-Mar-1994	28-Sep-1994

	EOI partner	Type of agreement	Signature	Entry into force
21	Colombia	DTC	27-Jul-2010	03-Jul-2014
22	Cook Islands	TIEA	31-May-2011	05-Mar-2012
23	Costa Rica	TIEA	12-Oct-2016	13-Nov-2018
24	Croatia	DTC	13-Nov-2002	15-Sep-2006
25	Czech Republic	DTC	27-Apr-1992	03-Mar-1995
		DTC	12-Jan-2018	20-Dec-2019
26	Denmark	DTC	11-Oct-1977	08-Jan-1979
27	Ecuador	DTC	08-Oct-2012	16-Oct-2013
28	Egypt	DTC	09-Dec-1992	15-Jan-1994
29	Estonia	DTC	23-Sep-2009	25-May-2010
30	Ethiopia	DTC	26-May-2016	31-Oct-2017
31	Fiji	DTC	19-Sep-1994	11-Feb-1995
32	Finland	DTC	08-Feb-1979	23-Dec-1981
33	France	DTC	19-Jun-1979	01-Feb-1981
34	Gabon	DTC	25-Oct-2010	02-Dec-2015
35	Georgia	DTC	31-Mar-2016	17-Nov-2016
36	Germany	DTC	10-Mar-2000	31-Oct-2002
37	Greece	DTC	20-Mar-1995	10-Jul-1997
38	Guernsey	TIEA	23-Sep-2015	21-Dec-2016
39	Hong Kong (China)	DTC	08-Jul-2014	27-Sep-2016
40	Hungary	DTC	29-Mar-1989	01-Apr-1990
41	Iceland	DTC	15-May-2008	23-Oct-2008
42	India	DTC	19-Jul-1985	01-Aug-1986
		DTC	18-May-2015	12-Sep-2016
43	Indonesia	DTC	10-Nov-1988	03-May-1989
44	Iran	DTC	06-Jul-2006	08-Dec-2009
45	Ireland	DTC	18-Jul-1990	27-Dec-1991
46	Israel	DTC	18-Mar-1997	13-Dec-1997
47	Italy	DTC	10-Jan-1989	14-Jul-1992
		DTC (Protocol)	03-Apr-2012	02-Mar-2015
48	Japan	DTC	08-Oct-1998	22-Nov-1999
49	Jersey	TIEA	21-Jul-2015	21-Nov-2016
50	Jordan	DTC	22-Jul-2004	28-Mar-2005

	EOI partner	Type of agreement	Signature	Entry into force
51	Kazakhstan	DTC	18-Oct-1997	09-Apr-1999
52	Kenya	DTC	08-Jul-2014	03-Apr-2017
53	Kuwait	DTC	05-Dec-1998	13-Jun-2000
54	Kyrgyzstan	DTC	11-Dec-2012	22-Nov-2013
55	Lao People's Democratic Republic	DTC	29-Nov-2004	09-Feb-2006
56	Latvia	DTC	15-Jun-2008	26-Dec-2009
57	Lithuania	DTC	20-Apr-2006	14-Jul-2007
58	Luxembourg	DTC	07-Nov-1984	26-Dec-1986
		DTC (Protocol)	29-May-2012	04-Sep-2013
59	Malaysia	DTC	20-Apr-1982	02-Jan-1983
60	Malta	DTC	25-Mar-1997	21-Mar-1998
61	Marshall Islands	TIEA	31-May-2011	09-Mar-2012
62	Mauritius	TIEA	11-Aug-2016	13-Apr-2017
63	Mexico	DTC	06-Oct-1994	11-Feb-1995
64	Mongolia	DTC	17-Apr-1992	06-Jun-1993
65	Morocco	DTC	27-Jan-1999	16-Jun-2000
66	Myanmar	DTC	22-Feb-2002	04-Aug-2003
67	Nepal	DTC	05-Oct-2001	29-May-2003
68	Netherlands	DTC	25-Oct-1978	17-Apr-1981
69	New Zealand	DTC	06-Oct-1981	22-Apr-1983
70	Nigeria	DTC	06-Nov-2006	Ratified by Korea
71	Norway	DTC	05-Oct-1982	01-Mar-1984
72	Oman	DTC	23-Sep-2005	13-Feb-2006
73	Pakistan	DTC	13-Apr-1987	20-Oct-1987
74	Panama	DTC	20-Oct-2010	01-Apr-2012
75	Papua New Guinea	DTC	23-Nov-1996	21-Apr-1998
76	Peru	DTC	10-May-2012	03-Mar-2014
77	Philippines	DTC	21-Feb-1984	09-Nov-1986
78	Poland	DTC	21-Jun-1991	21-Feb-1992
		DTC (Protocol)	22-Oct-2013	15-Oct-2016
79	Portugal	DTC	26-Jan-1996	21-Dec-1997
80	Qatar	DTC	27-Mar-2007	15-Apr-2009
81	Romania	DTC	11-Oct-1993	06-Oct-1994

	EOI partner	Type of agreement	Signature	Entry into force
82	Russia	DTC	19-Nov-1992	24-Aug-1995
83	Samoa	TIEA	15-May-2015	22-Nov-2016
84	Saudi Arabia	DTC	24-Mar-2007	01-Dec-2008
85	Serbia	DTC	22-Jan-2016	17-Nov-2016
86	Singapore	DTC	06-Nov-1979	11-Feb-1981
		DTC (Protocol)	24-May-2010	28-Jun-2013
		DTC	13-May-2019	31-Dec-2019
87	Slovak Republic	DTC	27-Aug-2001	08-Jul-2003
88	Slovenia	DTC	25-Apr-2005	02-Mar-2006
89	South Africa	DTC	07-Jul-1995	07-Jan-1996
90	Spain	DTC	17-Jan-1994	21-Nov-1994
91	Sri Lanka	DTC	28-May-1984	20-Jun-1986
92	Sudan	DTC	10-Sep-2004	Ratified by Korea
93	Sweden	DTC	27-May-1981	09-Sep-1982
94	Switzerland	DTC	12-Feb-1980	22-Apr-1981
		DTC (Protocol)	28-Dec-2010	25-Jul-2012
95	Tajikistan	DTC	31-Jul-2013	28-Sep-2016
96	Thailand	DTC	16-Nov-2006	29-Jun-2007
97	Tunisia	DTC	27-Sep-1988	25-Nov-1989
98	Turkey	DTC	24-Dec-1983	27-Mar-1986
99	Turkmenistan	DTC	13-Apr-2015	26-Nov-2016
100	Ukraine	DTC	29-Sep-1999	19-Mar-2002
101	United Arab Emirates	DTC	22-Sep-2003	02-Mar-2005
		DTC	27-Feb-2019	Ratified by Korea
102	United Kingdom	DTC	25-Oct-1996	30-Dec-2006
103	United States	DTC	04-Jun-1976	20-Oct-1979
104	Uruguay	DTC	29-Nov-2011	22-Jan-2013
105	Uzbekistan	DTC	11-Feb-1998	26-Jun-2006
106	Vanuatu	TIEA	14-Mar-2012	08-Jun-2017
107	Venezuela	DTC	26-Jun-2006	15-Jan-2007
108	Viet Nam	DTC	20-May-1994	09-Sep-1994

Convention on Mutual Administrative Assistance in Tax Matters (amended)

The Convention on Mutual Administrative Assistance in Tax Matters was developed jointly by the OECD and the Council of Europe in 1988 and amended in 2010 (the Multilateral Convention).[29] The Multilateral Convention is the most comprehensive multilateral instrument available for all forms of tax cooperation to tackle tax evasion and avoidance, a top priority for all jurisdictions.

The original 1988 Convention was amended to respond to the call of the G20 at its April 2009 London Summit to align it to the international standard on exchange of information on request and to open it to all countries, in particular to ensure that developing countries could benefit from the new more transparent environment. The Multilateral Convention was opened for signature on 1 June 2011.

Korea signed the Multilateral Convention on 27 May 2010 and it entered into force on 1 July 2012 in Korea. Korea can exchange information with all other Parties to the Multilateral Convention.

As of 27 April 2020, the Multilateral Convention is in force in respect of the following jurisdictions: Albania, Andorra, Anguilla (extension by the United Kingdom), Antigua and Barbuda, Argentina, Aruba (extension by the Netherlands), Australia, Austria, Azerbaijan, Bahamas, Bahrain, Barbados, Belgium, Belize, Bermuda (extension by the United Kingdom), Brazil, British Virgin Islands (extension by the United Kingdom), Brunei Darussalam, Bulgaria, Cameroon, Canada, Cayman Islands (extension by the United Kingdom), Chile, China (People's Republic of), Colombia, Cook Islands, Costa Rica, Croatia, Curaçao (extension by the Netherlands), Cyprus,[30] Czech

---

29. The amendments to the 1988 Convention were embodied into two separate instruments achieving the same purpose: the amended Convention which integrates the amendments into a consolidated text and the Protocol amending the 1988 Convention which sets out the amendments separately.
30. Note by Turkey: The information in this document with reference to "Cyprus" relates to the southern part of the Island. There is no single authority representing both Turkish and Greek Cypriot people on the Island. Turkey recognises the Turkish Republic of Northern Cyprus (TRNC). Until a lasting and equitable solution is found within the context of the United Nations, Turkey shall preserve its position concerning the "Cyprus issue".

    Note by all the European Union Member States of the OECD and the European Union: The Republic of Cyprus is recognised by all members of the United Nations with the exception of Turkey. The information in this document relates to the area under the effective control of the Government of the Republic of Cyprus.

Republic, Denmark, Dominica, Dominican Republic, Ecuador, El Salvador, Estonia, Faroe Islands (extension by Denmark), Finland, France, Georgia, Germany, Ghana, Gibraltar (extension by the United Kingdom), Greece, Greenland (extension by Denmark), Grenada, Guatemala, Guernsey (extension by the United Kingdom), Hong Kong (China) (extension by China), Hungary, Iceland, India, Indonesia, Ireland, Isle of Man (extension by the United Kingdom), Israel, Italy, Jamaica, Japan, Jersey (extension by the United Kingdom), Kazakhstan, Korea, Kuwait, Latvia, Lebanon, Liechtenstein, Lithuania, Luxembourg, Macau (China) (extension by China), Malaysia, Malta, Marshall Islands, Mauritius, Mexico, Moldova, Monaco, Montserrat (extension by the United Kingdom), Morocco, Nauru, Netherlands, New Zealand, Nigeria, Niue, North Macedonia, Norway, Pakistan, Panama, Peru, Poland, Portugal, Qatar, Romania, Russia, Saint Kitts and Nevis, Saint Lucia, Saint Vincent and the Grenadines, Korea, San Marino, Saudi Arabia, Senegal, Serbia, Seychelles, Singapore, Sint Maarten (extension by the Netherlands), Slovak Republic, Slovenia, South Africa, Spain, Sweden, Switzerland, Tunisia, Turkey, Turks and Caicos Islands (extension by the United Kingdom), Uganda, Ukraine, United Arab Emirates, United Kingdom, Uruguay and Vanuatu.

In addition, the Multilateral Convention was signed by the following jurisdictions, where it is not yet in force: Armenia (enters into force on 1 June 2020), Benin, Bosnia and Herzegovina, Burkina Faso, Cabo Verde (enters into force on 1 May 2020), Gabon, Kenya, Liberia, Mauritania, Mongolia (enters into force on 1 June 2020), Montenegro (enters into force on 1 May 2020), Oman, Paraguay, Philippines, Togo and United States (the original 1988 Convention in force on 1 April 1995, the amending Protocol signed on 27 April 2010).

Annex 3: Methodology for the review

The reviews are based on the 2016 Terms of Reference and conducted in accordance with the 2016 Methodology for peer reviews and non-member reviews, as approved by the Global Forum in October 2015 and the 2016-21 Schedule of Reviews.

The evaluation is based on information available to the assessment team including the exchange of information arrangements signed, laws and regulations in force or effective as at 27 April 2020 (the "cut-off date"), Korea's EOIR practice in respect of EOI requests made and received during the three year period from 1 January 2016 to 31 December 2018, Korea's responses to the EOIR questionnaire, information supplied by partner jurisdictions, as well as information provided by Korea's authorities during the on-site visit that took place 9 to 11 December 2019 in Seoul and Sejong, Korea.

Laws, regulations and other material received

Banking and AML/CFT laws

Commercial laws

Tax laws and EOIR Manual

Administrations and organisations interviewed during the on-site visit

Financial Services Commission

Financial Supervisory Service

Korea Federation of Banks

Korea Financial Investment Association

Ministry of Economy and Finance

National Tax Service

Ministry of Justice and the Register Office

Representatives of financial institutions

Current and previous reviews

Korea previously underwent an EOIR peer review in 2012, conducted according to the ToR approved by the Global Forum in February 2010 (2010 ToR) and the Methodology (2010 Methodology) used in the first round of reviews. Information on each of Korea's reviews are listed in the table below.

Review	Assessment team	Period under review	Legal framework as of	Date of adoption by Global Forum
Round 1 Combined 2012 Report	Ms Merete Helle Hansen of Denmark; Mr Kamlesh Varshney of India; Mr Bhaskar Goswami of India; and Mr Rémi Verneau of the Global Forum Secretariat.	1 January 2008 to 31 December 2010	January 2012	November 2013
Round 2 2020 Report	Ms Alexandra Kadet of Russia; Ms Talei Esera of Samoa; and Ms Kaelen Onusko of the Global Forum Secretariat.	1 January 2016 to 31 December 2018	April 2020	August 2020

Annex 4: Jurisdiction's response to the review report[31]

Korea would like to give thanks for the hard work of the assessment team and the Global Forum Secretariat, and the Peer Review Group for evaluating Korea's EOIR process.

Korea is committed to promoting tax transparency by exchange of information for tax purposes. Since the last peer review in 2012, Korea has expanded and improved the framework of exchange of information. Korea signed the MCAA and implemented FATCA, the Common Reporting Standard and Country-by-Country reporting. Korea also has expanded EOI network greatly, exchanging information with 148 jurisdictions through bilateral agreement, MAC and TIEA.

Korea amended the domestic tax law in 2019 in order to meet the revised 2016 TOR and thereby strengthening the availability of beneficial ownership information. The National Tax Service (NTS) is also monitoring and effectively in control of beneficial ownership information.

In regards to EOIR practice, the NTS established a new computerized EOIR system in 2016 that significantly improves its timeliness by systematic monitoring. All incoming requests (100%) that Korea had received were updated with a 90-day status.

Korea respects the Peer Review Group's efforts to ensure that issues relating to horizontal equity are properly taken into consideration as part of the evaluation process. Korea also recognizes the review process should be respected in all steps along the way to fully reflect assessed jurisdiction's position.

Korea will continue to make an effort to ensure effective exchange of information.

---

31. This Annex presents the Jurisdiction's response to the review report and shall not be deemed to represent the Global Forum's views.

www.ingramcontent.com/pod-product-compliance
Lightning Source LLC
LaVergne TN
LVHW070445070526
838199LV00037B/697